Early Childhood Staff Orientation Guide

Early Childhood
STAFF
Orientation
GUIDE

Sharon Bergen, PhD

Redleaf Press®
www.redleafpress.org
800-423-8309

Published by Redleaf Press
10 Yorkton Court
St. Paul, MN 55117
www.redleafpress.org

First edition 2016
Cover design by Ryan Scheife, Mayfly Design
Cover photograph © Rawpixel.com/Shutterstock.com
Interior design by Ryan Scheife, Mayfly Design
Typeset in the Sirba and Adoquin typefaces
Printed in the United States of America
23 22 21 20 19 18 17 16   1 2 3 4 5 6 7 8

Library of Congress Cataloging-in-Publication Data
Names: Bergen, Sharon.
Title: Early childhood staff orientation guide / Sharon Bergen.
Description: St. Paul, Minnesota : Redleaf Press, 2016.
Identifiers: LCCN 2015043414 | ISBN 9781605544311 (paperback)
Subjects: LCSH: Early childhood education. | Child development. | BISAC:
  EDUCATION / Preschool & Kindergarten. | EDUCATION / Reference. | EDUCATION
  / Professional Development.
Classification: LCC LB1139.2 .B47 2016 | DDC 372.21—dc23
LC record available at http://lccn.loc.gov/2015043414

Printed on acid-free paper

CONTENTS

————————

ACKNOWLEDGMENTS

this book would not be possible without the support, suggestions, and hard work of many people. I particularly want to acknowledge the many centers directors who have participated in the Directors' Credential learning community through Eager to Learn. Individually, and as a group, you encouraged the ideas that led up to the development of this book. Also, your enthusiasm for mentoring others and welcoming new staff members into the early childhood profession has been an inspiration throughout the development process.

I also want to acknowledge, and profoundly thank, the hardworking team at Redleaf Press. This book was improved greatly by your guidance, edits, and patience. Thank you to Christine Zuchora-Walske, whose thoughtful editing made a huge difference in the final product. Equally, thank you to Laurie Herrmann and Kara Lomen, who were steadfastly dedicated to this project and provided valuable cheerleading and support.

INTRODUCTION

Congratulations! You have chosen an important, exciting, and challenging profession.

Early childhood education is important work because children have only one chance to get the best possible start in life. During their early years, children are rapidly developing, and the environments, interactions, and activities in which they engage make a big difference in how and to what extent development occurs. You make a big difference in how a child in your care develops.

Working with young children is also exciting. Young children are playful and fun-loving. Interacting with them can be joyful and can offer you a chance to see the potential in each child and in our future as a community. You have the opportunity to make each day fun for the children and fun for you as well.

Working with young children is physically and intellectually challenging work, too. Children depend on the adults around them to care for them and to make decisions that protect their health and safety and support their potential for development and learning. You will find that each day you must be constantly on your toes to keep up with the children physically and mentally.

Alexander Graham Bell, inventor of the telephone, is often credited with having said, "Before anything else, preparation is the key to success" (Lederer 2011, 6). This sentiment applies well to early childhood education. You probably selected this career because you are fond of children or because you consider yourself good at interacting with children. But liking children or having an interest in children is not all you will need to be successful. You'll also need a solid preparation for the complicated and important work of caring for children.

This *Early Childhood Staff Orientation Guide* is designed to give you that preparation and start you on your professional journey. Each chapter contains loads of information about best practices for working with young children. These practices are designed to protect children's health and safety and to support positive development of the whole child. Whether you are starting your first job working with children or you bring previous experience to this role, you will find both new and familiar ideas within this guide. Often early childhood professionals base their ideas on their own childhood experiences or observations of others interacting with children. Some of the ideas in this guide will reinforce what you already know. Some of the ideas may contradict your previous experiences or challenge your prior notions about caring for young children. All the ideas are based on best practices as defined by experts in early childhood education and by the profession's many regulations and standards. You'll reap the most benefit from this guide if you are open to blending new ideas with those you have already mastered.

About This Guide

The information in this guide is organized into an introduction, four chapters, and a list of resources. Throughout each chapter you will find helpful information on best practices in the care and education of young children. You will also find opportunities to apply what you are learning in the reading to the unique setting in which you have chosen to work. This feature is structured in the form of a list of questions and tasks. It is recommended that you talk with and observe others who are carrying out the best practices described in each chapter. At the end of each chapter are questions to help you check your learning and apply what you know. Your employer will appoint an Orientation Mentor to walk alongside you through this work. Your Mentor will help you determine the order in which you should tackle the sections of this guide. Your Mentor will also help you learn the practices that are specific to the program and the classroom to which you are assigned.

Chapter 1: About Young Children

Decades of research have resulted in vast amounts of information about how children grow and develop as well as some of the behaviors common to each age or stage of development. Chapter 1 presents general information about child development and the practices associated with each age or stage of development. This chapter also describes the way in which professionals interact with young children and their families and the guidance techniques that are appropriate to early childhood programs.

Chapter 2: Protecting Children's Health and Safety

The young children in your care rely on you to keep them safe and well. This chapter gives information about the prevention of children's illnesses and injuries. It also addresses preparation for emergencies.

Chapter 3: A Day in the Program

Although each day you work with young children will be unique in some ways, other aspects of the day will remain consistent and predictable. This chapter describes each of the major parts of a typical day in an early childhood program. It includes best practices related to arrival, meals and snacks, diapering and toileting, outdoor play, naptime, learning activities, and departure routines.

Chapter 4: Being a Professional

With this orientation, your professional journey is just beginning. Chapter 4 gives you a chance to work with your Orientation Mentor to plan for your

The Orientation Mentor

The National Association for the Education of Young Children (NAEYC) describes mentoring as "a relationship-based process between colleagues in similar professional roles, with a more-experienced individual with adult learning knowledge and skills, the mentor, providing guidance and example to the less-experienced protégé or mentee" (NAEYC and NACCRRA 2011, 10). Your employer will assign one experienced colleague from your program to be your mentor during your orientation to work in this program. Your Orientation Mentor will support you in getting to know the program's rules of the road.

The *Early Childhood Staff Orientation Guide* lists a wide variety of questions you can discuss with your Mentor about the way things happen in your program. It also suggests practices that you should observe your Mentor conducting and, in some cases, practices that your Mentor should observe you conducting. This strategy is intended to give you the information and models you need to master the skills associated with best practices in an early childhood program. But do not limit yourself to the questions and directions in this guide. You may ask your Orientation Mentor additional questions or ask her to demonstrate or observe other practices. If your Mentor is not able to answer your questions, she will arrange for additional support to meet your needs.

professional development beyond your orientation period. This chapter also addresses various aspects of professionalism in early childhood education.

Resources

This guide contains only enough information to get you started in your work with young children. It touches on many topics that may pique your interest. The resources section lists sources of information on some of these topics that you can seek out on your own for further learning.

Limitations

The *Early Childhood Staff Orientation Guide* is designed to offer you a broad introduction to the best practices in early care and education. But its scope is limited in some ways. A guide of this type cannot possibly address every topic of importance to the care and development of young children. It addresses some topics only briefly; other topics are outside its scope. The selection of topics for this guide follows the recommendations found in the NAEYC program accreditation criteria and those suggested in *Caring for Our Children: National Health and Safety Performance Standards; Guidelines for Early Care and Education Programs, Third Edition*. Since the topics in this guide are meant to be introductory, you will need ongoing professional development so that you can continue to grow in your role.

The content of this guide is based on best practices across the profession. It may not fully address the individual regulations and regional requirements defined by state and local licensing and regulatory agencies. The guide makes every attempt to include opportunities for gathering information about the specific regulations that apply to your program. But, ultimately, it is your responsibility to know and comply with all the regulations in your location.

Terms

The early childhood profession is full of interesting terms and acronyms. Often different terms refer to the same thing, or people use terms with little attention to actual meanings. Use of terms in this guide may not match the way these words are used in your area or in your program. To prevent confusion, the following list defines the meanings of several key terms as they are used in this guide:

- *Early childhood education* or *early childhood profession*: These phrases refer to the broad field of work that encompasses child care, preschool, and other settings in which young children (from birth to kindergarten entry) receive care and education.

- *Teacher*: This term refers to everyone who works directly with young children, providing care and education for them. It includes all the varying levels of teachers, assistants, aides, and other roles. This choice honors the role that everyone in the lives of young children plays in teaching important skills and supporting development.

- *Program*: This term refers to the organization or site where you work. For example, ABC Child Care Center is a program. This term includes child care centers, family child care programs, preschools, school-based programs, and other sites where young children receive care and education.

- *Classroom*: This term refers to the individual space within the larger program where you work. A very small program may have only one classroom. But most programs have multiple classrooms, often separating children into age groups. For example, your program may have an infant classroom, a toddler classroom, and a preschool classroom. Family child care programs may not think of or refer to their spaces as classrooms, even though a great deal of learning occurs within the walls of these environments. But for simplicity's sake, this guide refers to individual spaces within all programs as classrooms.

- *Director*: This term describes the person with the lead administrative or supervisory responsibility for a program. In most programs, teachers report to the director.

- **Pronouns**: This guide alternates between male and female pronouns to denote teachers and children.

Helpful Documents

As you work through this guide, you will find it helpful to have a few resources on hand. These resources may be paper or electronic documents. Work with your Orientation Mentor to gather the following:

- licensing regulations
- staff handbook or other documents that include or refer to program policies or procedures
- family handbook or other documents that include or refer to program policies or procedures
- program curriculum

Apply Your Knowledge

Throughout each chapter of the *Early Childhood Staff Orientation Guide* are features titled "Apply Your Knowledge." These sections should be completed in collaboration with your Orientation Mentor. The questions or tasks described are meant to provide a framework for a conversation between you and your mentor. You might think of the questions as a short interview that you will conduct with your Orientation Mentor. In this interview you will ask the questions and your mentor will help you to complete the answers. By asking and answering the questions and completing the tasks described, you will learn how the ideas presented in this book are applied in the specific program in which you work. The questions will help you to determine where materials are located, how program-specific policies are structured and implemented, and the basic "rules of the road" for the unique program in which you have chosen to work.

Check Your Learning

Each chapter of the *Early Childhood Staff Orientation Guide* ends with a short quiz. This quiz gives you an opportunity to show what you have learned about various aspects of your program and about working with young children. Use the quiz as a learning tool. If you are unsure about some questions, take a few minutes to review the guide's corresponding information. Or spend some time with your Orientation Mentor reviewing the relevant best practices. Remember, your goal is to feel well prepared. Use the quiz as one indicator of your readiness.

CHAPTER 1

About Young Children

What comes to mind when you think about young children? Do you picture a child who is fun-loving? Warm? Creative? Busy? Lovable? Cute? Do you recall times when young children you know were frustrating or even difficult? All these descriptions, and many more, can apply to young children. Children, like adults, are often lovable and fun to be with. And sometimes they will challenge your patience and make your role as a teacher and caregiver difficult.

Decades of research have given our profession a solid understanding of the developmental norms for children of varying ages or stages of development. We know a lot about what an infant, a toddler, or a preschooler is likely to do. But a child is more than just a set of research-based expectations. Children also have unique personalities, needs, interests, and behavior patterns. Over time you will get to know the actual children in your care, and you will be able to predict many of their behaviors based on their developmental abilities and their individual characteristics. Yet even when you have this knowledge and experience, children may surprise you from time to time! This is one of the fun aspects of working with young children. They can be unpredictable, and their changing developmental abilities and moods make each day unique.

You probably chose this profession because you like children. A fondness for children is a great start—but it's just a start. Understanding how children develop will help you work with them effectively. This knowledge will make

Domains of Development

Child development is a broad and complex topic. To make discussion more manageable, the many aspects of development are often organized into domains. Commonly discussed domains of development are motor or physical development, cognitive or intellectual development, social and emotional development, and language development. As children grow, they develop in all these areas simultaneously. In fact, the domains are so intertwined that development in one area affects development in another area. For example, to reach an important developmental milestone such as toilet learning (potty training), children must have the physical development necessary for bowel and bladder control. They must also have the cognitive development to understand when their bodies are signaling the need to use the toilet, and they must have the language ability to ask for help in using the toilet. Mastering use of the toilet influences children's emotional development because they experience great pride in their ability to do such a grown-up task.

your job easier, and it will help you support children's growth and learning more successfully.

The pages that follow address general principles of child development and some of the developmental expectations associated with infants, toddlers, and preschoolers, as well as the practices used in early childhood programs based on these principles and expectations. If you have already studied child development, some of this information will be a review. If you have spent a great deal of time around young children, you will see these ideas about development come alive as children play and learn in your care.

Child Development Basics

Knowledge of typical behavior for children of various ages is helpful to an early childhood educator. This knowledge helps you anticipate what children can do and helps you minimize risks to their health and safety. For example, since you know that infants are likely to put any objects they can grasp into their mouths, you also know that it's a good idea to keep sharp items or small items that could cause choking away from babies. Similarly, you know that older preschoolers enjoy the challenge of playing with small blocks and that they are unlikely to mouth toys, so it's okay to provide small blocks for them. Your knowledge of child development helps you decide what materials to have in your classroom, what activities to plan, and how to interact with the children.

During the first few years of life, children grow and change dramatically. Picture a newborn baby. The baby is all wiggles and reflexes and relies on his caregivers to meet even his most basic needs. Now picture the same child as a five-year-old, ready to board the bus for kindergarten. This child is quite independent; he feeds himself, walks easily, speaks his mind, makes friends, chooses games and activities, and more. A lot of development has occurred in five short years! The development that occurs in early childhood is predictable in many ways, and fortunately, we know a lot about how teachers like you can best support this development.

Principles of Development

A discussion of every theory and principle of child development is beyond the scope of this guide. But some basic principles of child development serve as the foundation of all we do in early childhood programs. A brief summary of these ideas will familiarize you with the assumptions about child development that underlie the information you will cover in your orientation.

PREDICTABLE SEQUENCE OF DEVELOPMENT

One of the most important principles of child development is that development typically occurs in a predictable way. You can make some assumptions about what children of various ages can do based on your knowledge of these predictable stages. For example, think about writing. You can predict that an infant will have little writing ability. She may be able to make simple marks on a page with a crayon, but she is not yet able to make recognizable letters or numbers. Likewise, you can predict that the same child at four years old will be able to make some marks that resemble letters or numbers. If the child has had access to crayons or other writing tools, she may be able to copy letters or words and write letters that are part of her name. This example illustrates just two points in a predictable sequence of writing development for young children. Other aspects of development—walking, talking, imaginative play, and so on—also follow predictable sequences. These sequences have been well researched and well documented in the child development literature.

Notice in the preceding example the words "if the child has had access to crayons or other writing tools." This phrase illustrates another important principle in child development: experiences matter. A child's development is only partly a matter of maturation. It can only proceed in the typical orderly sequence if the child has opportunities to develop and practice skills. For example, imagine a one-year-old child who is just starting to learn how to walk. If that child has plenty of chances to pull himself up, cruise along while holding on to low furniture, and fall safely from time to time, he will likely learn to walk by about twelve to fifteen months. But if that child is routinely in a swing, chair, or other restraining device and rarely or never has access to a safe place to practice walking skills, his walking development could be greatly delayed. The opportunity to experiment, practice, and explore with appropriate space, materials, and support from a caring adult like you makes a huge difference in whether the typical developmental sequence occurs.

The predictable sequence of development does not tell us everything we need to know about an individual child's development. The sequence tells us the order in which various skills are likely to occur and how development builds over time. But the rate of development is not always predictable. For example, we know that most babies do some form of rolling, then crawling, then cruising before walking; however, we do not know the exact age at which each of the behaviors will appear. Some babies take their first steps very early, at eight or nine months. Other babies are in no rush and take those first steps after their first birthday. Learning to walk anytime within this range is considered typical development.

The predictable sequence of development can take place unevenly among a child's various abilities. For example, a child who was an early walker and took her first steps at nine months may not necessarily achieve other developmental milestones early just because she walked early. The child who was an early walker may be a late talker and may not say her first words until after her first birthday.

Influences on the Sequence and Rate of Development

A child's experiences are just one factor influencing the rate at which the child progresses through the sequence of development. Other factors can affect how development occurs, too. First, special learning needs or medical or physical conditions may influence a child's development. For example, a child with Down syndrome, a form of cognitive impairment, will likely accomplish many developmental milestones at a slower pace than children without this condition. At some point, you will probably work with children who have special needs, as most early childhood programs today are inclusive. An inclusive program includes children with a wide variety of special educational, medical, or learning needs alongside children who are developing typically. In inclusive programs, all children's needs are met by adapting the program's activities and interactions to each child's level of development.

Second, a child's development is influenced by the child's culture and the context in which the child is growing and learning. In its position statement on developmentally appropriate practices, NAEYC defines the term *culture* as "the customary beliefs and patterns of behavior, both explicit and implicit," that a society—or a social, religious, or ethnic group within it—teaches its members (NAEYC 2009, 13). All people have a culture and are influenced by it, even if they are somewhat unaware of the impact because culture is such an ingrained part of their everyday lives. For example, a child growing up in a culture that highly values cooperation is less likely to strive for a strong sense of independence. This child's behavior will be subtly influenced by the value his family and community put on cooperative behaviors. Similarly, a child growing up in a family that highly values athletic endeavors is likely to have many early experiences in athletic activities and many chances to practice motor skills. There is a good chance that this child will strive for mastery of physical skills to please those around her. These factors combined may speed up her development of some physical skills and will also influence her interests and preferences.

PRACTICAL TIP: Developmentally Appropriate Practice

The phrase *developmentally appropriate practice* is used frequently in the early childhood profession. Carol Copple and Sue Bredekamp, in their book *Basics of Developmentally Appropriate Practice*, say that "developmentally appropriate practice refers to teaching decisions that vary with and adapt to the age, experience, interests, and abilities of individual children within a given age range" (2006, 7). This means that when you are teaching in developmentally appropriate ways, you are matching your knowledge of the typical expectations for a child's development and your knowledge of each individual child to what you do in your classroom. Using developmentally appropriate practice means that you select materials and activities that challenge the child and stretch his development, but are not so challenging that the activity is frustrating or dangerous to him. Using developmentally appropriate practice also means that you are intentional about what you do—that you plan and carry out activities and interactions with children in a thoughtful way, with a purpose in mind.

Third, decades of research support the idea that play is the best vehicle for development. When playing, children engage with materials and people in a hands-on way, using their senses and budding thinking skills to solve problems, make decisions, learn concepts, and develop relationships. Playful experiences that look like simple fun are actually important skill-building opportunities. When children's basic needs are met and they feel safe enough to play, they can build relationships with you and other adults and children, try new activities, experiment, and even fail. Through these actions and interactions, children learn about the world around them, develop new skills, and grow prepared for the demands of school and life.

Infants

Don Herold, an American humorist and writer, once said, "Babies are such a nice way to start people" (Robertson 1998, 168). There is nothing cuter than a baby. Infants have an innate ability to make us smile and inspire us to cuddle them and help them, which is important because they depend on others for their care and survival. Although newborns are helpless, they are quickly acquiring a wide range of skills. In fact, infants are undergoing a period of rapid growth that includes critical brain development, physical development, social and emotional development, and even language development.

Different agencies and authorities define the term *infancy* differently. For the purposes of this guide, infants are children from birth to one year old.

When you're working with infants, you can typically expect the following classroom needs and responsibilities:

- **Infants will be on individual schedules of eating, sleeping, eliminating, and playing.** You will need to keep track of each infant in your care and work closely with the child's family to understand her needs.

- **Babies will signal their needs by crying, not by speaking.** Babies are just beginning to learn language. They can listen to and understand some words eventually, but they do not start using words until around their first birthday. Babies will not be able to tell you what they need. You will need to be a detective to find out whether a crying baby is wet, hungry, tired, or just bored.

- **Infants will explore their environment through their senses, often using their mouths.** Infants are in what developmental theorist Jean Piaget called the sensorimotor stage of development, when infants explore objects and people using their senses—especially the sense of touch. Infants like to hold things, put them in their mouths, and shake them. In response to this style of learning, you will need to babyproof the environment by eliminating anything toxic, sharp, and that has small parts or long strings. A baby-safe environment contains many items that infants can safely touch and taste while moving around and exploring freely.

- **Babies will rely on you to meet their needs and build relationships.** Developmental psychologist Erik Erikson believed that babies are at a stage of development in which they are seeking to develop trust in their world, including you and the other adults who care for them. Babies do best when they can count on you to respond quickly and behave predictably.

- **Infants will need supervised tummy time for play and exploration.** While much of the day in an infant classroom is devoted to the care routines of eating, diapering, and sleeping, infants also need free time in a safe area for exploration and movement. Infants rarely play with one another, but they do like to have different materials to touch, taste, make noise with, and enjoy. This playful exploration builds important connections, or neural pathways, in the brain and is essential to early development.

- **Babies will do best when you work closely with their families.** Caring for a baby requires a partnership between you and the baby's family. Since babies thrive on consistency and predictable routines, you must work closely with each family to communicate information about the baby's day, to ask questions, to problem solve, and to understand the family's preferences. This flow of communication will not only benefit the baby but will make your work easier and more gratifying.

During their first year, you can expect that many babies will develop in the following ways:

- They will roll over, crawl, sit up, cruise along furniture, and eventually walk unsteadily.
- Infants will cry, smile, gurgle, coo, babble, and eventually begin to say their first words.
- They'll grow their first few teeth.
- Babies will respond to sounds, move to music, and eventually imitate sounds.
- They will watch your facial expressions, copy you from time to time, seek your attention, and show interest in and respond to your words or facial expressions.
- Infants will grasp toys, hold and shake toys, put toys in their mouths, and eventually put simple toys together, drop items in a bucket, or empty a bucket of toys.

PRACTICAL TIP: Brain Development

When infants are born, they have many well-developed body systems. The infant's brain controls all the important survival reflexes, such as the sucking reflex. But the brain continues to develop after the infant's birth. Early experiences and relationships help infants develop neural pathways in the brain that conduct impulses. When infants have many positive experiences exploring the environment and building relationships with you and other caregivers in their lives, they build many strong neural pathways that their brains will use their entire lives. When you are a responsive caregiver who quickly and effectively attends to an infant's needs, you help build an infant's brain. Offering many chances for the infants in your care to explore, touch, taste, and be involved in sensory experiences also builds the infants' brains. All these positive experiences support babies' development today and in the future. For more information about the growing body of research on infant brain development, visit the website of Harvard University's Center on the Developing Child at http://developingchild.harvard.edu.

PRACTICAL TIP: Primary Caregiving

Trusting relationships and responsive interactions are crucial to healthy infant development. To support trusting relationships and responsive interactions, many infant classrooms use a practice known as primary caregiving, in which caregivers are assigned smaller groups of infants. For example, in a classroom of two teachers and eight infants, each teacher is assigned one primary caregiving group with four infants.

The primary caregiver takes responsibility for planning, communication, and documentation for his small group of infants. The primary caregiver is often the person who communicates with the family about the child's day, fills out daily information forms, or responds to e-mail messages from a family member. Primary caregiving is not an excuse to ignore the needs of a baby from another care group. Teachers in classrooms using primary caregiving still work cooperatively to ensure that all children get responsive care at all times.

APPLY YOUR KNOWLEDGE

Meet with your Orientation Mentor to gather information about the infant classroom in your program. Answer the following questions and complete the task described:

1. What is the ratio of children to adults in the infant room in your program?

   _____

2. How many infants are in an infant classroom?

   _____

3. Does the infant room use primary caregiving?

   _____

4. How do teachers track the eating, sleeping, and elimination of infants and communicate this information to families?

   _____

5. Are there any infants currently enrolled in the program who have identified special medical or developmental needs? If so, what are the needs, and what supports exist to provide appropriate care for these infants?

   _____

6. How do infant teachers learn about the cultural preferences, practices, or traditions of families using the program?

   _____

7. Tour an infant classroom with your Orientation Mentor. Look for examples of the unique needs of infants and some of the developmental expectations during infancy.

   Initials _____

Toddlers

Toddlers are typically defined as children from one to three years old. The term *toddler* originates from the toddling, somewhat unsteady, gait of a child just learning to walk. Toddlers in your program may be divided into groups of younger and older toddlers. For example, it is common for programs to create separate classrooms for two-year-old children (older toddlers).

During the toddler years, young children are growing ever more mobile and are striving for independence. The combination of the toddler's desire to be independent and still-developing physical, social, emotional, and language skills make the toddler stage a challenging one. For example, toddlers have a strong desire to feed themselves and help set up and serve foods during meals. But their use of eating utensils isn't steady yet, so their attempts often result in spills, and sometimes in tears. As a teacher, you must allow toddlers to be as independent as possible so they can develop skills, but you must also be prepared for the inevitable cleanup duties that go along with budding self-help skills.

The toddler years are an interesting time when young children still have many of the same care needs of infancy but also begin to show the independence and mobility of preschoolers. In fact, it is tempting to treat toddlers as preschoolers because they want independence so strongly. But toddlers still need careful supervision and a great deal of individual attention. Many programs continue to use the infant practice of primary caregiving to help ensure that toddlers' needs are met.

When you're working with toddlers, you can typically expect the following classroom needs and responsibilities:

- **Toddlers will be on a more group-oriented schedule** and typically share mealtimes and naptimes. Some toddlers may still take a morning and afternoon nap, while others may take just one afternoon nap each day.

- **Toddlers will actively explore the environment and the materials** provided in the classroom. Like infants, toddlers are in the sensorimotor stage of development. They combine physical investigation with use of their senses to learn about their world. Toddlers will touch, taste, turn over, pound, carry around, throw, dump, and otherwise manipulate items to learn about them. Materials in the toddler classroom must be sturdy and safe for the children's active exploration.

- **Toddlers have a growing interest in social interactions.** They are more aware of other children and will, at times, try to play alongside and with others. But their social skills are still rudimentary. You can expect them to have a difficult time sharing and taking turns. Their friendships will seem very brief, and toddlers may appear to be selfish. These are typical behaviors for toddlers. They are not trying to be mean; they simply are not fully aware of others' feelings or how they should behave to get along with others.

- **Toddlers will experience an explosion of language.** Young toddlers are just beginning to use understandable words. The first words of infancy quickly develop into a working vocabulary of several hundred words by the time a toddler turns three years old. This growth in vocabulary and language depends on you. Since children learn language by hearing it, your modeling plays a critical role in how language develops for children in your care. You can support toddlers' language development by talking with them frequently, reading stories, sharing songs and rhymes, asking questions, and more.

- **Toddlers will sometimes be frustrated or upset and will act on those feelings in a physical way.** Part of learning to be independent is wanting to get your own way. Toddlers have a difficult time waiting or giving up their own desires for the needs of others. Sharing, taking turns, and other cooperative behaviors are difficult for toddlers, and when something is difficult, frustration and anger can result. Unfortunately, toddlers also have a challenging time understanding and responding to their own strong emotions. They will frequently act on these emotions physically by hitting, pushing, biting, and so on. You will need to address these behaviors firmly, while understanding that these actions are a typical part of toddler behavior.

- **Toddlers show curiosity and enthusiasm** for trying new things and engaging in fun activities. Toddlers find most activities interesting. They enjoy a wide range of play, including songs and games, building with blocks, painting and drawing, dressing up, running and climbing, and more. While toddlers do not focus on any one activity for very long, they do enjoy having a wide range of opportunities. You should plan many play choices for toddlers so they can select a variety of options throughout the day. Do not expect a toddler to linger at any activity for a long time. Moving on quickly does not mean that the child did not like the activity. In fact, he may return to it later after trying several other things.

- **Toddlers will be interested in you,** in what you are doing, and in engaging you in their play. Toddlers like to help and be involved with their teachers, and many toddlers find it easier to socialize with adults than with other toddlers. You can expect that toddlers will seek your attention and get frustrated if your attention is not available. You will need to be aware of all the toddlers in your group and ensure that you are spreading your time and attention among them.

During the toddler years, many toddlers will develop in the following ways:

- Toddlers will use understandable words and begin combining words in short two- to three-word sentences.

- They will walk with increasing coordination, begin to run (unsteadily at times), climb, learn to ride a scooter or tricycle, climb stairs with some support, sit and stand easily, throw balls, and jump up and down.

- Toddlers will learn to grasp crayons or markers with a fist (usually not with a pencil grip), stack objects easily, put together simple knob-type puzzles, and use large interlocking blocks or other building toys.

- They will hold cups and spoons or forks, pour liquid from a pitcher (with occasional spills), and eat independently. They may need help with opening and closing packages or with cutting foods.

- Toddlers will learn to open doors, unbutton large buttons, unzip zippers, untie shoes, take off their own coats, put away clothes and toys (not always neatly), and bring plastic dishes to the table.

- They will show interest in using the toilet, express upset with being wet or soiled, and may begin to use the toilet regularly.

- Toddlers will ask for familiar stories and songs.

- They will sing along during songs, name characters in familiar books, point out colors or familiar objects, and ask and answer questions about pictures and stories.

- Toddlers will remember familiar people and their names and will notice when they are absent.

PRACTICAL TIP: Biting

Biting is one common challenging behavior associated with the toddler years. Toddlers have a hard time verbalizing their wants and needs. And strong emotions are still confusing to them—even overwhelming at times. Biting is often a toddler's normal reaction to life's little frustrations. But even though biting is typical behavior, you should not ignore it or allow it to continue. To prevent and address biting, you should use the following strategies:

- Watch for signs that a child is becoming frustrated or upset, then step in to calm the situation.
- Avoid situations where toddlers may be overcrowded, overtired, or hungry for long periods of time.
- When biting occurs, first comfort and attend to the child who has been bitten, rendering first aid as needed.
- Firmly tell the child who has bitten, "No. We do not bite."
- Record the biting behavior using the tracking method employed in your program.
- Be prepared to work cooperatively with families if biting behavior continues or worsens over time.

APPLY YOUR KNOWLEDGE

Meet with your Orientation Mentor to gather information about the toddler classroom in your program. Answer the following questions and complete the task described:

1. What is the ratio of children to adults in the toddler room in your program?

   _____

2. How many toddlers are in a toddler classroom?

   _____

3. Is primary caregiving used?

   _____

4. How do teachers track the eating, sleeping, and elimination of toddlers and share this information with families?

   _____

5. How is biting behavior documented in the program? Who notifies families when biting occurs?

   _____

6. Are there any toddlers currently enrolled in the program who have identified special medical or developmental needs? If so, what are the needs, and what supports exist to provide appropriate care for these toddlers?

   _____

7. How do toddler teachers learn about the cultural preferences, practices, or traditions of families using the program?

   _____

8. Tour a toddler classroom with your Orientation Mentor. Look for examples of the unique needs of toddlers and some of the developmental expectations during the toddler years.

   Initials _____

Preschoolers

Preschoolers are typically defined as children who are three to five years old. In most programs, children remain in preschool classrooms until kindergarten entry. Since some children do not enter kindergarten until after they are six years old, your classroom may include preschoolers who are six years old. Children from three years old to kindergarten entry age are considered preschoolers because they have not yet entered formal education. However, preschool children are already learning and developing many of the important skills they will use throughout school.

Preschoolers are eager learners. They are generally very independent and curious. Unlike toddlers, preschoolers have a better understanding of social relationships and are better—but not perfect—at managing emotions and frustrations.

When you're working with preschoolers, you can typically expect the following classroom needs and responsibilities:

- **Preschoolers will conduct many self-help routines** with only minimal support from you. For example, most preschoolers are able to use the toilet, feed themselves, serve their own foods, take coats off and put them on, remove and put on shoes (although not tie shoes), wash hands (with reminders), blow their own noses, and request help when they need it.

- **Preschoolers' large-motor skills are flourishing.** They can run easily; jump; climb a short ladder; pedal riding toys; walk a short, low balance beam or plank; bounce and catch a large, soft ball; throw objects with some accuracy; swing on swings with a push to get started; and lift and carry objects such as boxes or large blocks.

- **Preschoolers will speak clearly** in short sentences of four to five words, use pronouns, ask and answer questions, make requests, and use language to persuade you to do something.

- **They can follow simple directions** and remember simple classroom rules from day to day.

- **Preschoolers will show interest in pretend play** with others, often dressing up or acting out familiar roles such as mommy, daddy, firefighter, dog, or others.

- **Preschoolers can listen to stories, songs, and rhymes and join in** when they hear familiar songs and rhymes.

- **They will create paintings, drawings, or other artwork**, showing creativity and pride in their work.

- **Preschoolers can manipulate objects** to play simple matching or sorting games.

- **They will stack and arrange blocks** to make complex structures and scenes.

- **Preschoolers will join friends in activities**, seek out familiar children, and attempt to take turns in games and activities (although not perfectly).

During the preschool years, you can expect that preschoolers will develop in the following ways:

- Preschoolers will achieve bladder control and use the toilet independently with few, if any, accidents. (They may still need reminders.)

- Preschoolers will master many, but not all, self-help tasks involved with daily eating, dressing, hand washing, and cleanup.

- They will speak fluently with a vocabulary of over one thousand words, combining words into sentences and using inflection for questions and statements.

- Preschoolers will say their own names and the names of a few familiar friends.

- They will name many colors and sort objects by their color.

- Preschoolers will name many objects and animals and sort them by categories, such as farm animals, zoo animals, and so on.

- They will count objects up to a set of ten and rote count using numbers higher than ten.

- Preschoolers will name a few letters, especially those in their own names.

- They will manipulate small blocks or connecting pieces, put together simple puzzles, and demonstrate increasing control of muscles in their hands by doing tasks such as lacing cards, stringing beads, or holding crayons or markers using a pencil grip.

- Preschoolers will listen to longer stories, retell familiar stories, and describe what is happening or predict what will happen next in stories based on pictures and other cues.

- They will draw simple shapes, letterlike forms, and pictures, with some recognizable objects, such as a tree, person, house, and so on.

PRACTICAL TIP: School Readiness and Academics

Preschoolers are beginning to show interest in subjects or content typically associated with formal education. For example, many preschoolers are starting to recognize numbers and letters and want to read and write. When these school-like behaviors start to appear, we may be tempted to transform the preschool into an elementary school classroom complete with lessons, worksheets, and the like. But this is not the best practice for young children and does not support their natural curiosity about academic subjects or their love of learning. Many early childhood programs do an excellent job of preparing children for school through playful, developmentally appropriate activities. Preschoolers should continue to learn through play, and you can support this learning by offering fun activities that also incorporate learning. For example, instead of using a worksheet about shapes, engage the children in tossing circle, square, and triangle beanbags into circle, square, and triangle boxes or baskets. The playful approach is more effective for young learners, who still do best when they are engaging their senses and acting on their ideas.

 **APPLY YOUR KNOWLEDGE**

Meet with your Orientation Mentor to gather information about the preschool classroom in your program. Answer the following questions and complete the task described:

1. What is the ratio of children to adults in the preschool room in your program?

   _____

2. How many preschoolers are in a preschool classroom?

   _____

3. How do teachers track the daily activities and learning of preschoolers and share this information with families?

   _____

4. Are there any preschoolers currently enrolled in the program who have identified special medical or developmental needs? If so, what are the needs, and what supports exist to provide appropriate care for these children?

    _____

5. How do preschool teachers learn about the cultural preferences, practices, or traditions of families using the program?

    _____

6. Tour a preschool classroom with your Orientation Mentor. Look for examples of the unique needs of preschoolers and some of the developmental expectations during the preschool years.

    Initials _____

Interacting with Young Children

Whether you are working with infants, toddlers, or preschoolers, most of your day will involve interaction with children. Interacting with children involves meeting their needs, playing alongside them, engaging them in conversation, suggesting activities, offering choices, and a host of other possible actions. In her book *The Intentional Teacher*, Ann Epstein says, "Children's interactions with teachers and peers, more than any other program feature, can determine what children learn and how they feel about learning" (2014, 18). How and when you choose to interact with the children in your care is a very important part of your teaching.

Perhaps you are thinking, "Interacting with children is the easy part of this job. I love children." In many ways you are right: it is fun, and sometimes easy, to interact with young children. But it takes thoughtful, or intentional, behavior on your part to ensure that your interactions with the children in your care support their positive development and potential for learning.

Intentional Behaviors

Like any other part of your teaching practice, interactions with children require thoughtful planning. This does not mean that you will plan everything you say to children or every moment you interact with them. That level of planning would be impossible and undesirable. Interacting with children in the moment is a better approach. In fact, taking advantage of events that occur spontaneously throughout the day, or teachable moments, is an important teaching strategy in working with young children. But you should carefully think through your overall strategy for interacting with children, the types of techniques you will use and actions you will employ. The following interaction techniques are some of the best practices for early childhood teachers:

- **Help children express needs and emotions.** Children feel emotions deeply, but they have a hard time talking about how they feel and what they need. You can support children with their social skills and emotional development by helping them learn an emotional vocabulary. Help children name their feelings, describe how they feel, or express what they want or need. It is not enough to simply tell children to "use their words" if they do not know what words to use. You can suggest emotion words that may fit the situation. For example, you might say, "You seem to be feeling angry. Does that sound right? What could we do to help you feel calm or happy?"

- **Acknowledge positive or prosocial behaviors.** Children tend to imitate behaviors that receive attention. When you notice and comment on positive, prosocial behaviors, such as helping, sharing, or waiting for a turn, you increase the likelihood that children will repeat these behaviors.

- **Give choices.** Like most adults do, children prefer to have a choice about what they do and how they do it. Giving children choices, even limited ones, helps them become more independent, supports their positive self-image, and increases the likelihood that they will behave cooperatively. Structuring choices in a way that helps children be successful is a learned skill. Offering a choice from two or three acceptable options helps children decide and prevents them from being overwhelmed. The question

"What do you want to do?" provides too many potentially over-whelming choices, and simply telling a child to go to the block area provides no choice at all. Instead, you can use a strategy of limited choices. For example, when you're starting play in learning centers, you might ask a child, "Would you like to play with blocks or play in the art center to get started this morning?"

- **Keep a consistent schedule and routine.** Children crave consistency and do best in a predictable environment. Your interactions with children can support a consistent schedule and routine. For example, singing a familiar cleanup song each time cleanup is needed reminds children which routine they should begin.

- **Ask questions and suggest ideas, strategies, or options.** Sometimes your interactions will help guide children's behavior; other times your interactions will help guide their thinking and discovery. Ask open-ended questions (those that require more than a one-word answer and that spark conversation) and offer suggestions, strategies, or options to get children thinking and help them make good decisions about behavior and learning. For example, when a child spills some water, you might ask, "What do you think you should do to prevent anyone from slipping?"

- **Model.** Perhaps you have heard the phrase "a picture is worth a thousand words." The same is true about a real-life picture: you! Your behavior, actions, words, and interactions with others all model for young children what you value and expect. Children are tuned in to your behavior. They notice what you do and do not do. If you sit on the tables but tell the children not to do so, they are more likely to do what you do, not what you say. Modeling kind, gentle interactions is one way to encourage children to be kind and gentle with one another.

- **Modify and adapt based on what you know about individual children.** Although children of the same age may be similar in many ways, each child is unique. You will need to use what you know about individual children in planning your interactions. Some children appreciate a gentle touch; some do not. Some children welcome your comments or questions; others like time to work quietly before you inquire about their work. Getting to know each child well will help you decide how and when to approach her and what kinds of comments, suggestions, and questions you should use.

Child Guidance

Young children are learning the behaviors necessary to get their needs met and to interact easily and happily with others. But developmentally, young children are still naturally focused on themselves. They are egocentric, meaning they tend to see situations from only their own point of view, considering primarily their own needs and wants. For example, when a toddler sees a toy he wants, it does not occur to him to think about the wants or needs of the child holding the toy. Instead, he focuses on his own desire for the toy and how he will get it. Because he is inexperienced in communicating with others, this child may simply take the toy rather than asking for a turn. The child does not behave in this way to be mean; he is actually acting in a way that is consistent with his level of development. However, this does not mean that teachers should let children hurt one another or engage in hurtful behavior that may come naturally to them. You are responsible for helping young children learn the rules of the road for interacting with others. Through your guidance, children learn how to participate in, and even enjoy, social interactions. They learn which behaviors are socially acceptable and which are not. They learn the consequences of behaving in ways that hurt others physically or emotionally.

Most early childhood programs have rules about the type of child guidance, or discipline, that can and cannot be used in the program. These rules may be listed in licensing regulations or may be developed by the program. It is essential that you fully understand the guidance strategies that are suggested for your program and those that are prohibited. Most programs prohibit any form of physical punishment or any action that could be considered emotionally abusive.

Strategies

In addition to having a complete understanding of forbidden guidance strategies, you must have several strategies you *can* use in your interactions with children to help them decrease challenging behaviors (such as hitting, pushing, or biting) and increase prosocial behaviors (such as helping, sharing, and turn taking). The following sections briefly describe strategies often used in early childhood programs. Over time you will learn to use each of these strategies and more to support the social and emotional development of the children in your care.

Prevention

One of the best ways to address challenging behaviors is to prevent them from occurring. Fortunately, you can do a lot in developing your environment and in planning activities to prevent challenging behaviors:

- **Provide enough space in group areas and learning centers** so that children are not crowded or forced to play too near one another all the time. Sometimes you may need to limit the number of children who can use a play area or learning center at the same time. For example, you might say that only three children can use the sensory table at the same time. This tactic minimizes the need to fight over space or supplies while playing.

- **Provide enough choices of materials and provide duplicates of popular toys or materials.** Young children are still learning to share and take turns, so it is wise to minimize waiting. For example, having two or three of the same popular truck in the block area or sandbox minimizes disputes over the toy.

- **Create a well-balanced daily schedule and stick to it as much as possible.** Young children crave predictability and are most likely to behave as we wish when they know what to expect from the day. Chapter 3 includes additional information about the daily schedule and the major parts of each day in an early childhood program.

- **Take care of basic needs—food, water, and rest—in a timely manner.** Children can control their emotions and impulses most easily when they are feeling well. So when children are well fed, hydrated, and well rested, their behavior improves. Staying on schedule with meals, snacks, frequent drink breaks, and rest times decreases the likelihood of challenging behavior.

- **Create and consistently follow a few simple, positively worded classroom rules.** Most children want to please you and want to behave in the way that is expected in the classroom. But children do not automatically know what behaviors are expected of them in a group setting. Choosing a few simple rules that briefly explain classroom expectations helps children learn how to get along in a group. For example, your classroom rules might include "Be kind" and "Ask for what you need with words." These positively stated rules remind children what they should do, rather than focusing on what they should not do.

- **Talk about being part of a group.** Take advantage of opportunities to talk about behaviors that are desired in your group. For example, read books about sharing or turn taking. Discuss classroom situations during group time so that everyone knows the expectations for new situations, equipment, or events.

- **Stay close to areas or activities where challenging behavior often occurs.** Sometimes your presence is all children need to remind them of the expected behavior. And when you are close to the action, you can quickly step in to redirect or distract children before problems occur. For example, if you know that the art easel is a popular area where children often have trouble waiting for a turn or sharing supplies, position yourself near this area to prevent and quickly defuse problems.

- **Build loving relationships with children.** All children develop best in a context of warm, responsive relationships. When children know they can count on you for warmth, affection, and stability, their behavior improves. Children who feel secure tend to feel good about themselves and interact easily with others. If children feel ignored or insecure, they may use challenging behaviors as a way to seek attention or connection.

- **Plan engaging activities.** When children have plenty to do, and when the activities available to them are interesting and fit well with their level of development, they are less likely to engage in challenging behaviors. Conversely, when children are bored or uninspired, they may take part in challenging behaviors for stimulation.

Despite all your prevention activities, challenging behavior will occur from time to time. This is a natural part of children's development, and you should expect it. When challenging behaviors do occur, use the strategies that follow and reconsider your prevention strategies. Reflect on changes you could make in the environment, schedule, interactions, or activities to minimize the chances of the behavior occurring again.

Redirection or Distraction

One of the benefits of children's short attention spans is that children are easily distracted or redirected to another activity. For example, when a toddler wants the toy someone else is playing with, it is usually easy to distract her with another equally interesting toy. Redirection also works well when children are starting down a problematic path and need a bit of help making a better choice. For example, imagine a preschooler is playing at the water table. You notice he is beginning to swirl the water and that if he continues, it will splash over the sides of the table. You could step in and redirect his interest in swirling water toward a less messy activity in keeping with the rules of using the water table. You might suggest that he add some water to a plastic bottle and see if he can swirl the water inside the bottle. This redirection subtly tells him that he may experiment with the water but may not splash the water outside of the water table.

Offering Suggestions, Alternatives, or Solutions

Young children have not yet developed logical thinking. They tend to act on impulse, without considering all the available options or the implications of their choices. And when children get involved in conflicts, their emotions sometimes prevent them from thinking of alternative actions or ideas that might resolve the conflict. You can help children resolve their conflicts by suggesting alternatives or solutions. For example, if two preschoolers both want to ride the same tricycle, you might ask, "What could we do to solve this problem?" If the children do not have any ideas, you could suggest, "Let's make a fair solution to this problem so both of you get an equal turn. What if Mia rides for five minutes, then Troy rides for five minutes?" In this suggestion the children hear an option for solving the problem that includes both children's need for a turn.

Calming the Situation

Young children are learning to understand and regulate their emotions. But this learning is a lifelong task, and they are just beginning. In fact, strong emotions such as anger are often overwhelming for children. Sometimes what children need most is some help stepping away from an emotional situation so they can take a moment to calm down and reconsider the situation. For example, imagine that two children are arguing over the police hat in the dramatic play (dress-up) area. Both children are upset and appear set on getting their own way. You might suggest, "Let's put the hat away for a while and read a story together. Later, when we are feeling calmer and ready to play again, we can go back to the dress-up area."

Engaging Help

Most of the time, strategies such as those described above are enough to decrease challenging behaviors and to guide children toward prosocial behaviors. But sometimes problem behaviors persist or even worsen over time. When this happens, it is important to engage help from others: colleagues, families, and sometimes experts. Keep the following principles in mind as you guide children with persistent challenging behaviors:

- **Follow your program's policies and consult your supervisor.** It is essential to be aware of and follow your program's policies for addressing persistent challenging behaviors. Knowing the policies will prevent you from promising something you cannot deliver or suggesting an action you cannot carry out. Your program's policies should help you know when and how to involve families and when and how to involve your supervisor. You should also use your supervisor as a resource any time you are unsure how to handle a child's behavior. Your supervisor can help you think through prevention techniques as well as strategies for responding to challenging behavior when it occurs or persists over time.

- **Document your observations.** When children do not appear to be responding to typical guidance strategies, take notes. Write down what has happened as well as the strategies you've tried and the reaction. These notes will help you find patterns in the child's behavior. Behavior patterns might suggest actions you could take to decrease the behavior. For example, you might find that a child who seems to hit others does so primarily before naptime. You might change the daily schedule somewhat to prevent the child from becoming overtired.

- **Ask your colleagues for their perceptions and suggestions.** Sharing your concerns or questions about a child's behavior with your colleagues can be helpful. You may find that something you feel is a problem behavior is described by your colleagues as typical for the age group. Or your colleagues may share your concerns. Often more experienced colleagues have ideas you have not yet tried for addressing a child's behavior. They may have information about the child's development that you did not know. Problem solving with colleagues is not only helpful in addressing children's challenging behaviors, it is also a great way to grow your skills as a teacher.

- **Work with the child's family.** Supporting a child's social and emotional development is best done in partnership with the

PRACTICAL TIP: Self-Regulation or Self-Control

One important skill children develop during early childhood is self-regulation, meaning they learn to control their own behaviors. Initially, children count on adults to help them control their behaviors or resist the impulse to do something unacceptable. Adults provide reminders and redirection, make rules, and so forth to help children choose behaviors that fit their social situations. Over time, children need to take control of their own behavior so they can thrive in social situations such as learning in a classroom or playing with friends. They need to develop their memory so they can recall the rules of a situation. And they need to be willing to resist the impulse to do the wrong thing in favor of doing the right thing.

Since the world is full of distractions and appealing choices, making good decisions is hard for children. Even adults do not exercise self-regulation perfectly. Think of the last time you said something you should have kept to yourself. Your self-control slipped. Children's self-regulation improves over time and with practice in making choices, communicating, and being patient. But self-regulation is never perfect. You should expect children to make frequent mistakes in self-control. You will need to offer support for their emerging skills.

child's family. Because children thrive on consistency, it's helpful when rules, strategies, and consequences are similar at home and in the classroom. You don't need to share every time you redirect a child's behavior, but when a child's challenging behaviors are not responding to typical guidance, it is a good idea to communicate with the child's family about what you have observed, what you are doing, and what the next steps are. It is also critical to ask the family for their observations and perceptions. While the child may not be exhibiting the same behavior at home, the family may be able to share information about changes contributing to the child's situation, such as a new sibling, the death of a pet, a family move, and so on.

- **Involve experts.** Occasionally a child's behaviors are so challenging and so persistent that your program may need to engage the help of experts such as therapists, speech pathologists, play or art therapists, or special education teachers. Typically, the director will work with the child's family to determine if and when experts should get involved. Your role may be to share your observations with the experts to help describe the situation, and you may be involved in carrying out experts' suggestions. Experts can be valuable resources for your program and can provide wonderful learning opportunities for you personally.

 **APPLY YOUR KNOWLEDGE**

Meet with your Orientation Mentor to gather information about the way in which interactions, including child guidance, occur in your program. Answer the following questions:

1. What discipline actions do licensing regulations or program policies prohibit?

_____

_____

_____

2. What strategies does the program encourage for interacting with children and for guiding children's behaviors? Does the program have a written policy?

_____

_____

_____

_____

3. In what situations should you document children's challenging behaviors? Should you use a particular form or format?

_____

_____

_____

_____

4. In what situations should you inform families of their children's challenging behaviors? Should you use a particular type of communication or form?

_____

_____

_____

_____

5. In what situations might an expert's help be needed in observing or addressing a child's challenging behaviors? Who contacts these experts?

_____

_____

_____

_____

Ethical Considerations in Working with Children and Families

Working with young children is an important responsibility that involves routinely making choices that have serious consequences. Early childhood professionals must use their ethics, or understanding of right and wrong, to make decisions and to respond to the needs of children, families, colleagues, the program, and the community. These decisions are not always easy, but guidance exists to help you make informed and ethical choices.

NAEYC has crafted a well-known and often-referenced code of ethical conduct for the early childhood profession. The code describes the responsibilities of early childhood professionals to children, families, colleagues, and the community and society. The code also describes several principles that you should consider when working with children and families. This section gives an overview of three key principles: do no harm, protect confidentiality, and work in partnership with families and colleagues.

Do No Harm

You probably selected this career because you enjoy working with children and want to be a part of their growth and development. It may seem unnecessary, or even a bit strange, that NAEYC has an ethical principle stating, "Above all, we shall not harm children" (NAEYC 2011). But this is a foundational concept in the care and education of young children; it is the one ethical principle that trumps all others. This principle makes it clear that all your professional decision making must serve the children's welfare, that the children's needs come before everything else. This principle takes a broad view of what causes harm to young children and makes it clear that "we shall not participate in practices that are emotionally damaging, physically harmful, disrespectful, degrading, dangerous, exploitative, or intimidating to children" (NAEYC 2011). This principle means that you may sometimes need to make decisions that are unpopular or that require you to do things differently than you have in the past. You may find that you need to reevaluate some practices from your upbringing, the way you raised your own children, or things you did in a prior work environment because they are inconsistent with this principle.

Protect Confidentiality

As a teacher of young children, you will have access to a great deal of information about the children and their families. That information helps you care for the children and be consistent with and knowledgeable about the children's home environments. But the information comes with responsibility.

Professionals like you are responsible for keeping information about children and their families confidential. You should share information with other professionals in your program only when needed to provide consistent, high-quality care for the children. While your intentions may be good, you should generally avoid sharing information about a child or a family with anyone outside of that family, and you should consider doing so only after consulting your director for guidance. Sharing information unnecessarily with other families, other staff members, or friends is unprofessional and is engaging in gossip.

The NAEYC Code of Ethical Conduct provides guidance on confidentiality with the following principle:

> We shall maintain confidentiality and shall respect the family's right to privacy, refraining from disclosure of confidential information and intrusion into family life. However, when we have reason to believe that a child's welfare is at risk, it is permissible to share confidential information with agencies, as well as with individuals who have legal responsibility for intervening in the child's interest. (NAEYC 2011)

This principle extends to situations in which two or more families share custody of a child. Each family is entitled to privacy and confidentiality of the information it shares with the program. And each family has the right to expect open sharing of information about the child. As the child's teacher, your role is to support the child and to remain impartial if families are in conflict. Your director can provide helpful guidance when conflicts between families occur in your classroom.

Work in Partnership with Families and Colleagues

The care and education of young children requires teamwork and partnership. Rarely does one person take all the responsibility for a child's upbringing. Families count on you to be part of the team who supports their children's development. And you can count on families and your colleagues for support.

Creating a partnership with families and colleagues involves communication—but it's more than just communication. Partnership involves sharing power and decision making about what is best for the children. Partnership includes asking for and acting on information from others and involving others in planning for important activities, such as assessments. For example, if a concern arises about a child's development, you may observe the child and document the ways in which her development compares to what is typical for her age. You may also ask colleagues for suggestions to support the child's development and help in documenting the concerns you have. You may ask the family for thoughts on the child's development and how the child is progressing at home. Using all this information, you can work in partnership with your program and the family to decide whether additional observations, referrals to experts, or other strategies might further support the child's development.

All these principles—doing no harm, protecting confidentiality, and working in partnership—are core elements of the NAEYC Code of Ethical Conduct. The full code contains additional guidance for working with young children. For more information about the NAEYC Code of Ethical Conduct and resources related to carrying out the code, see page 150.

☑ CHECK YOUR LEARNING: CHAPTER 1

Answer the following questions about what you have learned in this chapter. When you have completed the questions, review them with your Orientation Mentor.

1. **True or false?** (Circle one.) Child development typically occurs in a predictable sequence of events.

   _____

   _____

2. **True or false?** (Circle one.) The sequence of development informs you about the order in which children's skills are likely to occur, but not necessarily exactly when each new skill will emerge.

   _____

   _____

3. Describe two factors that might influence the rate at which development occurs.

   _____

   _____

   _____

4. What is an inclusive program?

   _____

   _____

   _____

5. Describe two behaviors you can typically expect for each age group:

   _____

   _____

Infants

_____

_____

_____

_____

Toddlers

_____

_____

_____

_____

Preschoolers

_____

_____

_____

_____

6. Describe two interaction techniques or practices often used with young children.

_____

_____

_____

_____

_____

_____

7. Describe two preventive guidance techniques.

    _____

    _____

    _____

    _____

    _____

    _____

8. Describe two guidance strategies you can use to address children's challenging behaviors.

    _____

    _____

    _____

    _____

    _____

    _____

9. Describe two actions that you can take when challenging behaviors are persistent or worsening.

    _____

    _____

    _____

    _____

    _____

10. What ethical principle trumps all others?

_____

_____

_____

_____

CHAPTER 2

Protecting Children's Health and Safety

the most important—and perhaps most obvious—expectation placed on you when you work with young children is that you will protect their health and safety. Families entrust their children to you, expecting that you will keep them safe and meet their needs. Young children depend on adults to meet their needs and to keep them safe because they are not developmentally able to do these things for themselves.

Young children are just starting to develop the physical and cognitive skills required to make good decisions about personal safety and hygiene. For example, a toddler may recognize his feelings of hunger, but he cannot yet choose nutritious foods, prepare those foods, or make good decisions about hand washing and cleanup without help. With your help, the same toddler can participate in a nutritious and pleasant mealtime, serve some of his own foods, eat independently, wash his hands before and after eating, and even help with some of the meal preparations and cleanup.

Your first step in keeping children safe and healthy is knowing the children in your care. In chapter 1, you learned about the developmental stages associated with children of different ages. Understanding these stages helps you anticipate and recognize typical behaviors. But all children are unique human beings with their own temperaments, personalities, and needs. These unique traits greatly influence the ways in which you will ensure a safe and healthy experience in your program. For example, you must know which children in your care have allergies and what substances might trigger allergic reactions. You also need to know about medical or developmental conditions, special educational needs, diet restrictions or preferences, and custody arrangements that dictate who can interact with or pick up a child from your program.

APPLY YOUR KNOWLEDGE

Meet with your Orientation Mentor and gather information about the children in the classroom where you will work. Remember, this is confidential information; you may not share it with people who do not work with the child. Use the space below to list the name of each child, the child's unique need or condition, and any adaptation, modifications, or safety practices associated with caring for this child.

_____

_____

_____

_____

_____

_____

In addition to knowing the children in your classroom well, you can use many practices to create and maintain a safe and healthy program for the children. The following pages describe best practices for preventing illness and injury among young children in daily activities and in emergency situations. You may find that when you use these practices, you, too, are healthier and less likely to suffer an injury on the job.

Illness Prevention

When groups of children spend time together, the risk of illness increases because young children have not yet developed immunity to many illnesses and are not yet consistent in practicing good hygiene habits. No one likes to be sick—not you and certainly not the children in your care. Fortunately, you can do a lot to help prevent the spread of illness in your classroom. Frequent and thorough hand washing, cleaning, disinfecting, and sanitizing, as well as excluding ill children from the program, support a healthier environment for all.

Hand Washing

Caring for young children is a hands-on endeavor. For this reason, proper hand hygiene is essential to your health and the health of the children in your program. Experts suggest that thorough and frequent hand washing is the best way to reduce the spread of infection in child care environments.

FREQUENCY

The American Academy of Pediatrics (AAP), the American Public Health Association (APHA), and the National Resource Center for Health and Safety in Child Care and Early Education (NRC) suggest thorough hand washing for you and the children at the following times (2011):

- arrival for the day, after breaks, or when moving from one classroom to another
- before and after any of the following activities:
  - preparing food or beverages (including bottles)
  - eating, handling food, or feeding a child
  - giving medication or applying a medical ointment or cream
  - playing in water used by more than one person (including sensory table play)
  - diapering
- after any of the following activities:
  - using the toilet or helping a child use the toilet

> ▸ handling bodily fluids (mucous, blood, or vomit) from sneezing, from wiping and blowing noses, or from mouths or sores
>
> ▸ handling animals or cleaning up animal waste (including cleaning pet cages or feeding pets)
>
> ▸ playing in sand, on wooden play sets, or outdoors
>
> ▸ cleaning or handling garbage or soiled laundry

- any time hands look or feel dirty or sticky

Universal or Standard Precautions

The Centers for Disease Control and Prevention (CDC) has developed a set of procedures called universal or standard precautions to protect you and the children in your care from the spread of illness. These precautions say you should assume that any blood or blood-containing body fluids or tissue discharges (such as urine, feces, blood, saliva, nasal discharge, eye discharge, or vomit) could contain blood-borne pathogens. This means you should treat all blood and bodily fluids (except breast milk) that could contain blood with caution using the following measures:

- Avoid directly touching blood or bodily fluids that may contain blood. When blood or bodily fluids are involved, wear gloves for cleanup or to provide first aid.

- Clean up spills of blood or bodily fluids as quickly as possible. First, wipe up as much as possible using a disposable paper towel. Discard the paper towel immediately in a securely sealed or tied plastic bag. Then clean and disinfect the area, avoiding splashing or spreading any contaminated substances, using detergent, disinfectant, carpet shampoo, or steam cleaning, depending on the surface.

- Dispose of bandages, diapers, cleaning rags, or other materials that have come in contact with blood or bodily fluids in a sealed plastic bag. Remove these items directly to outdoor trash bins as soon as possible.

- Wash your hands immediately following any contact with blood or bodily fluids, even if you wore gloves.

- If you have direct contact with blood or bodily fluids, immediately report the incident to your supervisor.

Your program may require that you have further training on standard or universal precautions or on preventing the spread of blood-borne pathogens. Ask your Orientation Mentor about your program's requirements.

HAND-WASHING PROCEDURE

When you're washing your hands many times a day, it's tempting to do so casually and to minimize or even miss important steps. But washing your hands the right way is as important as washing them at the right times. Each time you or the children wash your hands, follow this procedure:

1. Make sure the required supplies are on hand: running water, liquid soap, and clean, disposable paper towels or single-use cloth towels.

2. Turn on warm (not hot) water.

3. Moisten hands with water and apply soap to hands.

4. Rub hands together vigorously out of the water stream until a soapy lather forms. Rub between fingers; around nail beds; along wrists, backs of hands, and palms; and under and around jewelry. Continue rubbing for at least twenty seconds.

5. Rinse hands under warm running water until they are soap-free. No visible dirt should remain. Leave water running.

6. Dry hands with clean, disposable paper towel or single-use cloth towel.

7. Shut off water taps using a disposable paper towel or single-use cloth towel.

8. Throw the paper towel in a lined trash can or place the single-use cloth towel in a laundry hamper.

PRACTICAL TIP: Increasing Hand-Washing Duration

When you're washing your hands numerous times during the day, it's easy to cut short the time spent scrubbing with soap. A good rule of thumb to help you to keep scrubbing for twenty seconds is to hum or sing the "Happy Birthday" song two times. You can also teach children this fun technique to prolong hand-washing time.

PRACTICAL TIP:
Hand Sanitizers and Antimicrobial Soaps

Alcohol-based hand sanitizers can be used in place of soap and running water when running water is not available. For example, hand sanitizers are convenient for use during outdoor play or while on field trips. Hand sanitizers should not routinely replace soap and running water. They are recommended only for children over twenty-four months of age and on hands that are not visibly dirty. (Sanitizers do not clean; they only sanitize.) Hand sanitizers are toxic if ingested, so bottles of hand sanitizer should never be accessible to the children or used by children without careful adult supervision.

Antimicrobial soaps are not recommended for use with young children, as they are no more effective than soap and water and may have adverse effects on young children. Premoistened towelettes are also not recommended in place of washing with soap and running water because they do not clean hands as effectively as running water and the action of rubbing hands together.

 APPLY YOUR KNOWLEDGE

Meet with your Orientation Mentor to gather information about the way in which hand washing is conducted in your program. Answer the following question and complete the tasks described:

1. Where are hand-washing supplies (liquid soap, hand sanitizer, disposable towels) located?

   _____

   _____

2. Locate the posting near the sink showing the hand-washing procedure.

   Initials _____

3. Observe your Orientation Mentor demonstrating the hand-washing procedure.

   Initials _____

4. Demonstrate the hand-washing procedure for your Orientation Mentor.

   Initials _____

Cleaning, Sanitizing, and Disinfecting

Spaces used by groups of young children get messy. You should expect—even encourage—this because young children need to explore materials with their senses, and they need to practice doing things independently. This means there will be frequent spills, splashes, and other messes to address. Some programs have staff members or contractors whose primary work is cleaning, sanitizing, and disinfecting the environment. These workers may clean daily or less often. But even with using cleaning services, some routine cleaning tasks will be part of your work with children. Most programs have developed a cleaning schedule that divides daily, weekly, and monthly cleaning tasks among staff members. Participating in these ongoing cleaning tasks not only helps keep the environment clean and healthy for you and the children, it is also a chance to model for the children the importance of caring for the classroom and working together as a community.

The words *cleaning*, *sanitizing*, and *disinfecting* are often misused. Their meanings are as follows:

- **Cleaning is removing dirt and debris by scrubbing or washing and rinsing.** Cleaning often involves soap and water and some kind of manual scrubbing or rubbing.

- **Sanitizing is using a product, such as a diluted bleach and water combination, that reduces germs.** Sanitizing is often used on surfaces where food is prepared or served, such as tabletops, high chairs, counters, and so on. Sanitizing is also used on toys that children mouth.

- **Disinfecting is using a product that destroys or inactivates germs.** Disinfectants are typically stronger or more concentrated than sanitizers. Disinfectants are used on surfaces where toileting or diapering takes places, such as changing tables, toilets, and bathroom surfaces.

It is important to use the correct products for each cleaning task and to follow the directions for mixing and using cleaning, sanitizing, and disinfecting products. All cleaning products must be out of children's reach at all times. It's a good idea to involve children in cleanup tasks, but they should never use toxic cleaning products.

All items children touch should be cleaned when they get soiled. For example, if a child soils a crib sheet by vomiting, you must clean the sheet and crib immediately. In addition to these obvious cleaning tasks, routine cleaning occurs on a schedule established by the program. The following list details some of the typical cleaning tasks associated with the care of young children.

Clean and sanitize these items before and after each use:

- food preparation surfaces (such as countertops) and appliances
- tables and high chair trays
- mouthed plastic toys

Clean and disinfect these items after each use:

- changing tables
- potty chairs

Clean and sanitize or disinfect these items daily:

- door and cabinet handles
- computer keyboards
- drinking fountains
- floors
- hand-washing sinks and faucets
- countertops
- toilets
- diaper pails

Clean and sanitize or disinfect these items weekly:

- machine-washable cloth toys and dress-up clothes
- plastic play equipment and toys
- cribs, cots, or mats
- crib, cot, or mat sheets; pillowcases; and blankets

PRACTICAL TIP:
Cleaning, Sanitizing, and Disinfecting Schedule

If your program does not already have a schedule of the cleaning, sanitizing, and disinfecting tasks required for a healthy child care environment, you can download one from NRC at http://cfoc.nrckids.org/WebFiles/AppendicesUpload/AppendixK.pdf.

APPLY YOUR KNOWLEDGE

Meet with your Orientation Mentor to gather information about the way in which cleaning, sanitizing, and disinfecting take place in your program. Answer the following questions and complete the tasks described:

1. Where are cleaners, sanitizers, and disinfectants mixed and stored?

    _____

    _____

2. Where is the cleaning schedule posted?

    _____

    _____

3. What cleaning tasks are part of your role?

    _____

    _____

4. Observe your Orientation Mentor cleaning and sanitizing food-service surfaces (tables, high chairs, and so on).

    Initials _____

5. Demonstrate cleaning and sanitizing food-service surfaces for your Orientation Mentor.

    Initials _____

6. Observe your Orientation Mentor cleaning and disinfecting diapering or toileting surfaces.

    Initials _____

7. Demonstrate cleaning and disinfecting diapering or toileting surfaces for your Orientation Mentor.

    Initials _____

PRACTICAL TIP: Clean as You Go

Teachers do many cleaning tasks once each day. Often teachers conduct these routine cleaning tasks at naptime or at the end of the day. This limits children's exposure to cleaning chemicals and prevents teachers from being distracted when they need to focus on the care of the children.

However, some cleaning does need to occur throughout the day. All day long, children make small (and sometimes big) messes. Children rarely remember to clean up after their play or when they make messes. Taking some time for cleanup as spills, splashes, and other messes occur helps keep the mess from spreading and helps keep children safe from slips and falls that can occur around puddles and spills. A tidy classroom inspires children to help with cleanup chores. Tidiness makes play more fun because children can find what they want when they want it. Also, a tidy classroom projects a more professional image to families and inspires their confidence in your abilities as a teacher.

But remember, do not let cleaning as you go distract you from supervising the children. Perform cleaning tasks only if you can do so while keeping a watchful eye on the children.

Excluding Ill Children

Practicing thorough and frequent hand washing and keeping the environment germ-free with diligent cleaning, sanitizing, and disinfecting practices will reduce the risk of illness. But these practices cannot eliminate illness. Some amount of illness is inevitable in any group of children.

Identifying ill children in your classroom is important for two reasons. First, ill children may need medical treatment, and quickly identifying symptoms that may indicate an illness allows you to contact families so that they can seek prompt medical care. Second, identifying a child who may be ill allows you to separate that child from healthy children and prevent the spread of the illness.

Health Checks

Carefully observing children can often help you identify a child who is not feeling well. As children arrive every day, take a moment to greet each child and to casually check for signs of illness. This routine practice allows you to identify potentially ill children before their family members have left for the day and before the children have come in contact with other children. The daily health check does not need to be intrusive or lengthy. The following practices are relatively fast and fit within a typical morning drop-off routine:

- Ask toddlers and preschoolers, "How are you feeling this morning?"
- Ask family members about their children's night and morning. For example, you might ask, "How was her sleep last night?" or "How is he feeling this morning?"
- Position yourself at the child's eye level and do a quick visual inspection. Look and listen for these symptoms:
  - ▸ labored breathing or coughing
  - ▸ rash, swelling, pale or yellowish skin, or itchy scalp
  - ▸ watery, crusty, or swollen eyes
  - ▸ flushed appearance or forehead or cheeks that are clammy or warmer to the touch than usual
  - ▸ listless or irritable behavior or a child that is more clingy or difficult than usual

Throughout the day, continue to watch for additional signs of potential illness. These include the following symptoms:

- loss of appetite
- frequent bathroom use
- lack of energy
- unusual irritability or sleepiness
- scratching
- complaints of aches and pains

These symptoms may not warrant excluding a child from the program, but they should alert you to keep a close eye on the child. If you observe these symptoms, alert your supervisor and make a decision about whether the child's family should be contacted.

Most programs do exclude children who exhibit any of the following symptoms of illness:

- fever of 101 degrees Fahrenheit orally or 100 degrees axillary (under the arm)
- diarrhea
- vomiting

PRACTICAL TIP: Immunizations

Immunizations are an effective means of preventing certain illnesses that can, in some cases, be very serious or even deadly. Childhood immunizations begin during infancy and continue throughout early childhood. Several agencies, including AAP and CDC, have established and published a recommended schedule for childhood immunizations. You can help prevent illness by encouraging the families of children in your program to get immunizations on schedule. Ask your Orientation Mentor how your program monitors immunization due dates and who communicates with families about upcoming immunization requirements.

- symptoms of contagious illness, such as chicken pox, impetigo, head lice, and so on
- symptoms of strep throat, such as complaints of a sore throat, rubbing ears, swelling, or redness
- unexplained rash (not diaper rash)
- abdominal pain or cramping

When Children Become Ill

When children are ill, you need to follow certain steps quickly and carefully to ensure the comfort and health of the ill child and to prevent the spread of illness among the healthy children. When you notice symptoms of illness, do the following:

1. Immediately provide first aid (if needed) and comfort the child. For example, if a child has vomited, comfort and clean the child, following procedures for contact with bodily fluids.

2. Make sure the other children are supervised and escort the ill child away from the healthy children. Your program should have a designated location for ill children to rest comfortably until family members can pick them up from the program.

3. Alert your supervisor. Decide who will contact the family. Clearly describe the symptoms you have observed.

4. Gather the ill child's belongings so that family pickup will be easy.

5. Reassure the child that you look forward to her returning to the classroom when she feels better.

APPLY YOUR KNOWLEDGE

Meet with your Orientation Mentor to gather information about the way your program addresses ill children. Answer the following questions:

1. What are the program guidelines for excluding ill children? Where are these posted or how are they given to families?

    _____

    _____

    _____

    _____

2. What illnesses require notifying other families of the risk of contagion? How are families notified and by whom?

    _____

    _____

    _____

    _____

3. Where do ill children rest until picked up by their families?

    _____

    _____

    _____

    _____

Medication

Administering medication to young children is serious business. Only staff members who have been trained to administer medication should do so. Ask your Orientation Mentor if medications are given at your program and, if so, who in your program is designated to administer medication.

Injury Prevention

Young children are just starting to develop the coordination and motor skills required for fluid movement and exploring the environment. (In other words, they're still a bit clumsy.) This means that sometimes the children in your care will slip, trip, or fall. They will also sometimes take risks or engage in dangerous behaviors because they do not realize the potential outcomes. Although some childhood bumps and bruises are inevitable, you can do a great deal to minimize the frequency and severity of injuries to the children in your care. Keeping young children safe involves maintaining a safe environment and being prepared for potential emergencies.

Safety Checks

Maintaining a safe environment for children requires constant vigilance. Over time, materials get misplaced, equipment becomes worn or damaged, and routine use of the environment can cause hazards to appear.

Start each day with a safety check of your classroom and any other spaces used by the children in your care. Your program may have a checklist to use. An effective check of the environment involves more than simply glancing around the space. You will need to walk around the entire indoor and outdoor space and also get down at the children's level to check for hazards that aren't obvious at adult height.

Whether or not your program uses a checklist, you should check at least the following each day:

- All cleaners, chemicals, and potentially toxic substances are stored in locked cupboards and out of children's reach. Medications are stored in areas inaccessible to children.

- Toys or equipment with sharp edges, broken pieces, or loose pieces that could be a choking hazard are removed.
- Hot surfaces or materials, including hot drinks, are out of children's reach.
- Equipment such as shelves, tables, chairs, and cribs are in good repair, are sturdy, and do not have loose pieces or joints.
- Walls or equipment (indoors or outdoors) are free of chipping paint or splintering wood.
- Carpeting and rugs lie flat and have no holes, frayed edges, or other tripping hazards.
- Furniture is against walls or secured to prevent tipping.
- Electrical outlets are covered, and electrical cords are secured in a way that prevents tripping or pulling appliances down from shelves or counters.
- Cords for window blinds are out of children's reach.
- Sharp items such as knives, box cutters, or other adult tools are out of children's reach.
- Purses, backpacks, and diaper bags are stored out of children's reach.
- First aid kits are readily available and stocked.
- Clear paths to outdoor exits exist (free of furniture, gates, or blockades).
- Exit lights are lit.
- Indoor and outdoor spaces are free of debris and hazards such as plastic bags or balloons.
- Outdoor play areas, including sandboxes, are free of animal feces or other signs of animal presence.
- Outdoor equipment is secured to the ground, has an adequate soft fall zone surrounding it, and is free of splinters, peeling paint, rust, sharp edges, or other hazards.
- Sidewalks are clear of sand and upheavals that could cause tripping.
- Outdoor play areas are free of holes, stumps, roots, protruding pipes, or other hazards.

APPLY YOUR KNOWLEDGE

Meet with your Orientation Mentor to gather information about the way in which your program conducts daily safety checks. Answer the following questions and complete the task described:

1. Does the program use a particular safety checklist? If so, where is it located? Who uses it, and how often? Who receives and files the completed checklist?

    _____

    _____

    _____

    _____

    _____

2. Use the program safety checklist or the items in the list above to conduct a safety check in your classroom.

    Initials _____

Supervision

Supervision is an important aspect of teaching. The work is often referred to as "watching the children." But of course, effective supervision is much more than just watching children. Effective supervision protects children's health and safety and requires your active involvement and diligence. When you supervise young children, your full attention must be on their actions, behaviors, movements, and needs.

Ratios and Group Sizes

Child care regulations typically define the number of children each adult can supervise legally. These regulations protect the safety of young children by ensuring that each child has enough adult attention and that each adult can reasonably attend to the number of children in his care.

The ratio of children to adults varies with the age of the children. Younger children require more individual care, so each adult can care for fewer children. Older children, who are more independent, require less individual care, so each adult can care for more children.

Licensing regulations may also limit the number of children that can be cared for in one group. Group size limitations are designed to support active supervision and to minimize health and safety risks to young children. Younger children tend to require smaller group sizes, and older children can often be cared for in larger groups.

Most regulations require a minimum square footage of floor space per child, so the size of your space affects your group size. Room size regulations promote safety. It is difficult for you to supervise children when they are overcrowded, and the risk of accidents, injuries, and illnesses increases.

NAEYC recommends ratios of children to adults, group sizes, and room sizes that are associated with best practices in early childhood programs. NAEYC's recommendations are similar to the recommendations made in *Caring for our Children: National Health and Safety Performance Standards; Guidelines for Early Care and Education Programs, Third Edition* listed below (AAP, APHA, and NRC 2011, 4).

Age of Children in Group	Maximum Child:Staff Ratio	Maximum Group Size
Up to 12 months	3:1	6
13 to 35 months	4:1	8
3 years	7:1	14
4 years	8:1	16
5 years	8:1	16
6 to 8 years	10:1	20
9 to 12 years	12:1	24

The ratios and group sizes in the preceding chart are recommendations based on research and best practices, and your program may choose to follow them. Your program is required to follow the ratios and groups sizes described in your licensing regulations, which may be less stringent.

There may be certain times of day when ratios or group sizes can vary from the typical guidelines. For example, some state regulations allow a different ratio or group size during naptime. However, this is not universally true, and you must know the rules that apply to your program.

Best Practices for Active Supervision

You are responsible for a safe environment for the children and, through your supervision, for protecting them from unnecessary risks throughout the day. The following practices will help you safely supervise the children and prevent injuries:

- **Be a positive role model.** As you supervise children, model safe behaviors, safe use of equipment, and safe interactions. The children will learn from your example and imitate it. For instance, if you expect the children not to sit on tables, you must also avoid sitting on tables.

- **Educate the children on safe use of materials and spaces.** When you introduce new toys or activities, clearly explain safe uses and actions to avoid. Reinforce any rules for use, including the safe number of children who can use a toy or participate in an activity at one time.

- **Maintain the established ratios and class or group sizes at all times.** If you must step away from the children for a few minutes, make sure someone covers your role so supervision is consistent.

- **Avoid distractions.** Distractions such as phone calls, conversations, planning, and even cleaning limit your ability to fully and actively supervise the children. Save phone calls and conversations with colleagues for break time or other times when you are not supervising the children. Supervising children outdoors requires your full attention, too. Avoid conversations with colleagues or any other distractions during outdoor playtimes. Limit cleaning and planning tasks to times when the children are less active, such as naptimes, or to times when you are not responsible for supervising children.

- **Use teamwork.** When you are working alongside a colleague, divide supervision duties to provide the safest environment for the children. Agree on areas of the classroom or play yard that each of you will supervise. Avoid clustering with other staff. This practice often results in distraction and prevents you from focusing fully on the children's needs.

- **Identify areas of greatest risk or challenge.** Certain areas of the classroom or play yard are more conducive to injuries. For example, the landing zone of the slide may seem to attract falls, bumps, and bruises. Areas where children can easily be out of sight, such as a tunnel within a play set, are also supervision challenges. Identifying these hot spots and watching them with extra vigilance can help you avoid many preventable injuries.

- **Establish and enforce classroom rules that support safe play.** Most classrooms have a few simple rules that remind children of safe behaviors and support positive interactions. Such rules help you maintain a safe environment and help everyone play together. Consistently mention the rules and acknowledge children who follow them. Typical rules may include some or all of these:

  - Walk when you're indoors.
  - Gently touch others and materials.
  - Be kind.
  - Replace what you use when you are done.
  - Take turns.

- **Conduct frequent attendance checks to account for all the children in your care.** This is particularly important during transitions. If you are moving children from one space to another, such as going outdoors to play, take a moment for a quick attendance check before you leave the classroom and once you're outdoors. You must know how many children, and which children, you are responsible for at all times. Frequent head counts help you maintain supervision of each and every child.

APPLY YOUR KNOWLEDGE

Meet with your Orientation Mentor to gather information about the way in which your program maintains supervision. Answer the following questions and complete the task described:

1. What are the ratios and group sizes mandated in your licensing regulations?

    _____

    _____

    _____

2. What are the ratios and groups sizes used by your program?

    _____

    _____

    _____

3. Do the regulations permit any variations in the ratios or group sizes? For example, what are the ratios and group sizes during naptime?

    _____

    _____

    _____

4. What is the maximum number of children permitted in the classroom where you will work, based on the size of the room?

    _____

    _____

    _____

5. How does your program monitor attendance and child count (the number of children in your care) throughout the day?

_____

_____

_____

6. Observe and help conduct a count of the children in the classroom where you will work.

Initials _____

Child Abuse Prevention

One type of childhood injury that is completely preventable is injury resulting from child abuse or neglect. It is hard to imagine that anyone would knowingly hurt a young child, but sadly, it does happen. The US Department of Health and Human Services estimates that there were 679,000 victims of abuse and neglect among children of all ages in the United States in 2013 (2015). The youngest children are the ones most likely to be victims of maltreatment. (*Maltreatment* is an umbrella term that includes both child abuse and neglect.) In addition to the obvious immediate physical harm it may inflict on children, maltreatment can also have long-lasting psychological effects. Fortunately, there is much that early childhood educators can do to prevent maltreatment and to ensure that maltreated children get immediate attention.

Professionals like you have two main responsibilities: reporting suspected maltreatment and ensuring that no children, including those in your direct care, are ever abused or neglected in your program. To fulfill these responsibilities, you must first be aware of what constitutes child maltreatment and know the signs that might point to maltreatment.

The Child Abuse Prevention and Treatment Act defines child abuse and neglect as, at a minimum: "any recent act or failure to act on the part of a parent or caretaker, which results in death, serious physical or emotional harm, sexual abuse or exploitation, or an act or failure to act which presents an imminent risk of serious harm" (US Department of Health and Human Services 2010).

Acts of child abuse and neglect fall into four categories: physical abuse, sexual abuse, psychological maltreatment, and neglect. A child may be the victim of maltreatment that falls into one or more of these categories.

SIGNS OF POSSIBLE ABUSE

Children of any age or ethnic group can be victims of maltreatment. Maltreatment occurs in families of all types and of all income levels. The signs of child maltreatment may be physical, such as bruises or burns, or they may be subtler behavioral changes. Teachers like you, who work directly with children, are in a good position to spot the signs that a child may be suffering maltreatment. Because you spend a great deal of time with children and get to know them well, you can notice changes in a child's behavior and, because the child trusts you, he may share his fears or concerns with you.

Physical Abuse

Young children naturally have occasional bumps and bruises from typical childhood accidents, such as falls. Physical abuse is when children sustain physical injuries from nonaccidental events. Physical abuse includes acts such as beating, burning, punching, kicking, biting, or otherwise physically attacking. Physical signs of child physical abuse include the following:

- bruises on areas of the body not typically associated with childhood falls, such as the abdomen, head, neck, backs of legs, forearms, or genitals
- bruises or marks with distinct shapes, such as handprints, belt buckles, cords, or rods
- unexplained injuries, such as adult-size bite marks, burns, bald spots, or broken bones or teeth
- repetitive injuries or injuries in various stages of healing

Behavioral indicators of physical abuse include the following:

- showing unusual fear of adults or reluctance at physical contact with adults or other children
- reluctance to go home
- being described as clumsy or accident-prone
- wearing out-of-season clothing to cover arms and legs (to conceal injuries)

Abusive Head Trauma or Shaken Baby Syndrome

Abusive head trauma (AHT), often referred to as shaken baby syndrome, is a form of physical abuse associated with infants. Experts estimate that 1,200 infants are seriously injured each year from AHT, resulting in at least 80 deaths (AAP 2015). Although AHT can occur in children up to five years old, victims are typically under one year old.

AHT often occurs when adults caring for babies are unable to control their frustration with a baby's consistent crying. When a frustrated or angry adult forcefully shakes a baby, the baby's head rotates uncontrollably, because the neck muscles are underdeveloped and the head has little support. This movement causes the baby's brain to move within the skull, potentially rupturing blood vessels, damaging brain tissue, and causing bruising and bleeding in the brain. Throwing or striking a baby in a way that causes the baby's head to hit a surface or an object can also cause AHT.

Signs of AHT in a child include the following:

- lethargy, difficulty breathing, or blue color due to lack of oxygen
- seizures, rigidity, or inability to lift head
- unconsciousness
- unequal pupil size or inability to focus the eyes or track movements
- vomiting, poor sucking or swallowing, or dramatic changes in appetite not due to other illness

AHT causes dramatic negative consequences, including possible death. Infants who have been victims of shaking, striking, or throwing need immediate medical attention. If you suspect that a child in your care is a victim of AHT, alert your director immediately so medical services can be called.

AHT, like all physical abuse, is completely preventable. To avoid the frustrations that can result from working with infants who sometimes cry inconsolably, you need to know many baby-calming techniques. When a baby cries, try the following:

- Check for a wet or soiled diaper and change it if needed.
- Feed or burp the baby.
- Offer a pacifier or teething toy.
- Check clothing to be sure the baby is not too warm or too cool or that clothing is not binding, scratching, or pinching the baby.
- Gently rock or sway while holding the baby close to your body.
- Sing or hum while holding the baby.
- Take the baby on a short walk outdoors, making sure she is dressed for the weather.
- Distract the baby with a toy, book, or change of location.

- being aggressive toward others or destructive toward oneself or others
- regularly complaining of headaches or stomachaches without a clear illness or other cause

Sexual Abuse

Child sexual abuse includes any adult sexual behavior with a child, such as fondling, intercourse, exhibitionism, exploitation, and pornography. Many people link sexual abuse of children to strangers, but children often know their abusers. The impacts of sexual abuse can be physical, but they also include psychological consequences related to betrayal and the lack of trust that can result from living in an abusive situation. Physical signs of sexual abuse include the following:

- problems with urination or recurring urinary tract infections or yeast infections
- pain, itching, bruises, bleeding, or discharge in genital, vaginal, or anal areas
- difficulty or pain in walking, running, or sitting
- venereal diseases
- torn, stained, or bloody underwear

Very young children may not have the vocabulary to explain or describe their sexual abuse. And they may have emotional or psychological reasons—such as fear, shame, or guilt—not to share what is happening to them. But even if sexually abused children are unable or unwilling to speak about their abuse, they may tell of it through their behavior. The following are some behavioral indicators of sexual abuse:

- compulsive interest in sexual activities or play that involves sexually inappropriate behavior, including mimicking sexual behavior the child has learned or observed

- destructive behavior toward self or others, including self-mutilation

- fearful behavior, including fear of adults of a particular gender, fear at naptime, and sudden fears in particular situations

- regressive behaviors, such as bed-wetting or -soiling or thumb sucking after the typical age for these behaviors

- sexual knowledge or behavior that is unusual for the age of the child, including drawing sexually explicit pictures, telling sexually oriented stories, or acting in a way that is suggestive or sexual toward others

Psychological or Emotional Maltreatment

Psychological or emotional maltreatment rarely occurs as a onetime event. It often accompanies other forms of abuse. Psychological or emotional abuse includes rejecting, belittling, ignoring, isolating, constantly criticizing, or stigmatizing a child. This type of maltreatment affects children in many ways and can have both short- and long-term physical impacts. Following are some of the physical signs of psychological or emotional maltreatment:

- eating or sleep disorders
- self-abusive or destructive behaviors, such as head banging, hair pulling, and so on
- speech disorders
- bed-wetting after the typical age for this behavior
- ulcers or physical failure to thrive with no clear medical cause

Following are some of the behavioral signs of psychological or emotional abuse:

- extreme swings in behavior, such as being very passive one moment and very aggressive the next
- fear of parents or other adults
- depression, frequent crying (beyond what is typical for age), withdrawal from social situations, or consistent isolation
- lack of expression or interest in activity a great deal of the time, including lack of confidence to do activities that are typical for the age group (frequent "I can't" statements)
- frequent temper tantrums after the age at which tantrums are typical

Neglect

Child neglect is a caregiver's inattention to a child's basic needs. It includes failure to provide food, shelter, medical care, clothing, or supervision that results in significant harm or the risk of significant harm to the child. Neglect is more difficult to detect than other forms of maltreatment because neglect does not, at least initially, leave obvious physical signs. But chronic neglect can cause results as serious as those of physical abuse. Following are some physical signs of neglect:

- poor physical development, such as height or weight well below the typical standard for the child's age
- limp, weak muscles not caused by a medical condition
- scaly or splotchy skin or skin that is consistently cold, dull, or pale
- routine inappropriate clothing for the weather
- chronic fatigue, listlessness, or dark circles under the eyes
- consistent poor hygiene

Reporting Abuse or Neglect

You may work for many years with young children and never see any signs of child maltreatment. However, you need to be aware of the signs and of your responsibilities for reporting suspicions of maltreatment so you'll be prepared if such a situation arises.

All adults who work with young children in early childhood programs are *mandated reporters* of child abuse and neglect. This means that if you observe signs of child maltreatment or if a child tells you about a situation in which maltreatment has occurred, you are legally required to report this information to the appropriate agency in your area.

PRACTICAL TIP: Reasonable Suspicions

As an early childhood professional, you are required, or mandated, to report reasonable suspicions of abuse. You are not required to have proof that the abuse occurred or any idea of who committed it. The agency that takes the report will determine how to investigate your report and will decide on the appropriate interventions for the situation. As long as you are making the report in good faith, with no intention to harm or defame another person, you are exempt from any legal penalty or negative legal consequences from making the report—even if investigation determines the suspicion was unfounded.

PRACTICAL TIP: Interviewing Children

Interviewing children who are possible victims of abuse or neglect is a specialized task. Do not attempt to interview or question children about possible maltreatment unless the investigating agency has specifically directed you to do so. Even well-intentioned questions can frighten children, cause them to withdraw, or confuse the facts of the situation, which could make the investigation more difficult.

In every US state and Canadian province, child care providers and others working closely with young children are mandated reporters. The specific requirements for reporting vary from state to state and province to province, and the names of agencies accepting reports may vary within your state. Typically, reporting agencies want as much of the following information as you can provide:

- name, age, and home address of the child
- names, phone numbers, and address of parents or guardians
- type of suspected abuse and description of the signs you observed
- your name, phone number, and address

In some cases, the agency may ask if you believe the child is in imminent danger or if you know the name of the person alleged to have committed the abuse. This information is not required to make a report but may be helpful in some situations. You are only obligated to share what you know and your reasonable suspicions. You may decline to answer questions that you do not feel you have enough information to answer.

APPLY YOUR KNOWLEDGE

Meet with your Orientation Mentor to gather information about the way in which your program handles reports of suspected child abuse and neglect. Answer the following questions:

1. To what agency do you report suspicions of child abuse?

   _____

   _____

   _____

   _____

2. What is the phone number and street address of the reporting agency?

   _____

   _____

   _____

   _____

3. What are the required timelines for reporting?

   _____

   _____

   _____

4. Does your program have any specific policies and processes for reporting? If so, what are they?

   _____

   _____

   _____

   _____

PREVENTING MALTREATMENT IN YOUR PROGRAM

Although most child maltreatment is committed by family members, children are sometimes the victims of abuse or neglect within early childhood programs. You can do a lot to ensure that maltreatment does not happen in any program with which you are associated. Many programs have policies in place to minimize the risk of maltreatment. It's essential that you are aware of and comply with your program's policies in these areas:

- **Employee screening:** All staff members must undergo thorough screening to ensure that they are well prepared to work with young children. Screening should include a check of professional and personal references, an interview, and a background check for convictions related to abuse and neglect.

- **Supervision:** All staff members must follow program policies for constant supervision of children, including sticking to child:staff ratios and maximum group sizes.

- **Child interactions and guidance:** All staff members must know and follow program policies that ensure staff treat children kindly and respectfully, even when they exhibit challenging behaviors.

PRACTICAL TIP: Recognizing Stress

Working with young children is a joyful job, but like any job, it comes with stresses. Stress can lead to actions that you may regret, so it is critical to recognize your body's signals that you need a break. The following behaviors are commonly associated with stress:

- shortness of breath
- tightness in the chest or abdomen
- clenched fists or jaw
- sweating, shaking, nervous tics, or involuntary trembling or movements
- difficulty making routine decisions or addressing routine problems
- feelings of despair or helplessness

If you find yourself feeling these symptoms, contact your director immediately to request a short break from your work. You may find that a brief walk, a drink of water, or even a brief rest helps you regain your composure.

- **Stress:** All staff members should ask for help when they feel overwhelmed or stressed.

- **Open communication:** All staff members should share with the program leadership any concerns they have about the behavior of any other staff member. Sharing concerns allows program leaders to ensure the safety and well-being of the children and to provide support for staff who may be struggling with job tasks or personal issues.

Emergency Preparedness

Despite your efforts to minimize risks to children's safety, emergencies can occur, requiring you to respond quickly and efficiently. Emergencies happen infrequently in early childhood programs, but it is important to be prepared for them. Your response in such difficult situations can help minimize injuries or prevent additional injuries.

Child injuries are one type of emergency that occurs from time to time in all programs. Injuries can result from routine play or from natural or human-caused disasters. Some disasters occur only in certain areas. For example, programs in California must prepare for potential earthquakes, while programs in the central United States must prepare for tornadoes. Other disasters, such as fires, could occur anywhere.

Child Injuries

A complete explanation of child first aid is beyond the scope of this guide. Everyone working with young children should have training in first aid and pediatric cardiopulmonary resuscitation (CPR). In addition, you need to be aware of a few simple injury-related procedures when you are working with young children.

Be prepared for emergencies by knowing the following:

- Know where the closest first aid kit is at all times.
- Know emergency phone numbers and where the nearest phone is at all times.

- Know any special medical needs of children in your care, such as allergies or chronic illnesses (diabetes, asthma, and so on).
- Know how to use any emergency equipment in your program, such as fire extinguishers, intercoms, and so on.
- Participate in emergency drills, such as shelter-in-place or evacuation drills.

When an injury occurs, remember the following:

- Act quickly and remain calm. Although it's normal to feel anxious when a child gets injured, your agitation may cause the children to panic.
- Reassure the children and remain with them until help arrives.
- Alert others for help.
- As needed, follow procedures for evacuation or sheltering in place.
- Do not move a severely injured child or give medication unless directed to do so by emergency services.
- If you have been trained in first aid, render it.
- Follow your program's procedures for notifying families of the injury.
- Complete any reporting required by your program.

Disasters

Some emergencies, such as natural or human-made disasters, cannot be predicted or prevented. Disasters like tornadoes, earthquakes, fires, or chemical spills typically call for one of two responses to ensure children's safety: evacuation or sheltering in place. In addition, you can prepare for disasters to minimize the risk of injuries if one occurs.

Preparation

Although you cannot predict when disasters will occur, you can do a lot to prepare for them:

- Conduct frequent drills for evacuation and sheltering in place (such as tornado or earthquake drills).
- Know your program's emergency plan for moving to evacuation sites, contacting emergency services, and contacting families.

- Know the locations of emergency supplies, such as earthquake or tornado kits, and first aid kits.
- Keep emergency evacuation routes and shelter-in-place areas clear and easily accessible.
- Secure furnishings that could easily tip over or fall during emergencies. Store heavy equipment on low shelves or on the floor. Place toys with wheels on low shelves or on the floor.

Evacuation

Some disasters, such as fires, require you to help children evacuate the building as quickly as possible. Take the following actions to prepare for evacuation:

- Know the evacuation routes from any areas used by the children in your care. Each space you use should display an evacuation map.
- Know where your group should gather after evacuating.
- Practice evacuation at varying times of day and varying days of the week.
- Keep attendance lists and emergency information where it will be easily accessible when you need to evacuate.

When evacuating, do the following:

- Remain calm and follow your program's procedures.
- Focus on the children, not the disaster. Your first responsibility is the children's safety.
- Gather the children and proceed quickly and calmly along the evacuation route.
- Take your attendance list and emergency information as directed in your program's procedures.
- Along the way, reassure the children with a calm voice.
- Take frequent head counts to ensure that your group stays together.
- When you arrive at the evacuation site, take attendance again, then engage the children in calming activities, such as songs, stories, and so on.
- Wait for direction before returning to the building.

PRACTICAL TIP: Expect the Unexpected

In emergency situations, children may not behave as you expect them to. For example, children often hide when they are scared, even though hiding is unsafe. Or children may simply refuse to evacuate when you direct them to do so. Practicing emergency procedures, such as evacuation, helps children be prepared and avoid panicking when a real emergency occurs. Practicing also gives you a chance to talk about all the things children can do to stay safe within the classroom. You can add safety to your curriculum. Activities such as reading stories about safety or acting out the "stop, drop, and roll" procedure give children a feeling of control in scary situations.

SHELTERING IN PLACE

In some disasters, evacuation would place the children in greater danger. For example, it would be very risky to leave the building during a tornado or other severe storm. During disasters such as storms, chemical spills, or earthquakes, it is typically best to shelter in place.

Do the following when you are sheltering in place:

- Calm and reassure the children.
- Move the children into your designated shelter area—usually an interior room away from windows, exterior doors, and other hazards.
- Account for all the children using your attendance list; continue taking frequent head counts.
- If falling debris is a danger, direct the children to duck and cover their heads. If possible, move children under sturdy furniture, such as tables, to protect them.
- Stay in the shelter area until you're instructed to move.

After any emergency, follow your program's policies for notifying families. Continue to reassure the children. Praise them for their helpfulness during the emergency.

APPLY YOUR KNOWLEDGE

Meet with your Orientation Mentor to gather information about the way in which your program handles emergency preparedness. Answer the following questions and complete the tasks described:

1. Where are the program's health and safety policies and procedures stored?

   _____

2. Where are first aid kits stored?

   _____

3. Who is responsible for inventory and restocking of first aid kits?

   _____

4. Where are fire extinguishers located?

   _____

5. Where are other emergency supplies, such as earthquake or tornado kits, stored?

   _____

6. Which staff members are trained in first aid and CPR?

   _____

7. Where are emergency numbers posted?

   _____

8. Where are evacuation routes or maps posted?

   _____

9. Where is the evacuation site for your classroom?

   _____

10. Where is the shelter-in-place area for your classroom?

     _____

11. How often are evacuation or shelter-in-place drills conducted?

     _____

12. Where is the children's emergency information stored?

     _____

13. Observe and assist in an emergency evacuation drill.

     Initials _____

14. Observe and assist in a shelter-in-place drill.

     Initials _____

✓ CHECK YOUR LEARNING: CHAPTER 2

Answer the following questions about what you have learned in this chapter. When you have completed the questions, check in with your Orientation Mentor.

1. List five times during the day when hand washing is required:

   _____

   _____

   _____

   _____

   _____

2. How long should vigorous rubbing continue during thorough hand washing?

   _____

   _____

   _____

3. List three items or areas that should be cleaned and either sanitized or disinfected after each use.

   _____

   _____

   _____

4. List three signs of potential illness that you can observe in a routine daily health check.

   _____

   _____

   _____

5. List three symptoms associated with potential illness that would lead to excluding a child from the program.

   _____

   _____

   _____

6. Describe three hazards to look for in a daily safety check.

   _____

   _____

   _____

7. What is the ratio of children to adults in the room where you are scheduled to work?

   _____

   _____

   _____

   _____

8. Describe three best practices in effective supervision of young children.

   _____

   _____

   _____

9. List three physical signs of child maltreatment:

_____

_____

_____

_____

_____

10. List three behavioral indicators of child maltreatment:

_____

_____

_____

_____

_____

11. What does it mean to be a mandated reporter?

    _____

    _____

    _____

    _____

    _____

    _____

12. List the two types of responses that are used in most emergency situations.

    _____

    _____

CHAPTER 3

A Day in the Program

One fun thing about working with young children is that each day is unique. Young children are somewhat unpredictable, and they are always growing and changing. You can't always anticipate how they will react to activities you plan or predict how long the events of each day might take. Even so, certain components of each day are consistent. Creating a daily schedule that's as predictable and consistent as possible is extremely important to you and the children for the following reasons:

- A predictable and consistent schedule helps the children know what to expect and what behaviors will be needed during each part of the day. Young children are learning to trust you, and being consistent and predictable throughout the day fosters trust. Trust is the basis of positive relationships and contributes to pro-social behavior.

- You will be better prepared for the day when you know what will happen, when it will happen, and what you need to do. When you feel prepared, the children sense that, and they, too, are less anxious and better able to enjoy the day.

- Families will better understand their children's day and the rhythm of the events in the program. When they understand these things, families can more easily partner with you, support your work, and plan for the children's time at home.

PRACTICAL TIP: Displaying a Daily Schedule

Many teachers post a written version of their daily schedule in a place that's visible to family members. This is one way to help families envision the children's day and understand the routines of the program. Some teachers also create a child-friendly version of the schedule to post in the classroom. A pictorial schedule, using simple pictures placed in order of the day's events, can remind children of what comes next throughout the day. Schedules like this are a good way to support children's need for consistency and predictability.

Once you've established a daily schedule, you'll still need to be flexible. Sometimes you will want to adjust your schedule to fit the children's interests or to incorporate a special event. Even a factor as simple as the weather may affect your schedule. For example, you may need to shorten outdoor play because of poor weather, or you may want to increase your outdoor time on the first warm day of spring. Think of the daily schedule as a flexible guide, not a firm contract.

This chapter will highlight the major parts of the day that occur in most programs. The timing of these events varies based on the ages of the children and the type of program. For example, a half-day program may serve only a brief morning snack, while a full-day program may serve as many as two meals and two snacks.

Some daily events must occur at particular times as dictated by the operations of the entire program. For example, most programs have a schedule indicating when various groups can use the play yard. This schedule prevents overcrowding, which could lead to accidents and injuries. Use of other common spaces, as well as mealtimes and program opening and closing times, may also have a firm schedule.

✎ APPLY YOUR KNOWLEDGE

- -

Meet with your Orientation Mentor to gather information about the current daily schedule in the classroom where you will work. Answer the following questions and complete the task described:

1. When do the program and my classroom open and close each day?

   _____

2. What are the mealtimes and snacktimes? Are these times flexible?

   _____

3. At what times do my children use the play yard? Are these times flexible?

   _____

4. What other daily events are firmly scheduled?

   _____

5. Locate a copy of the current daily schedule for your group. Review the schedule with your Orientation Mentor. Refer to this document as you read about each component of the day in the rest of this chapter.

   Initials _____

Arrival Routines

Most early childhood programs begin in the morning. In some programs, all the children arrive at the same time. In other programs, children arrive throughout the day. The staff schedule in your program reflects the anticipated arrival and departure times of the children. Depending on your program's schedule and your assigned shift, your workday may start after some of the children have arrived, or you may arrive before the children and have the chance to welcome each child.

The first few hours of each morning can be very busy. Teachers are typically preparing activities and materials for the day while children and their families are arriving. Often family members look forward to a few minutes of morning conversation with you to convey important information about the child's day. While these things are happening, the children also need constant supervision and leadership in their play activities. Juggling these competing demands can make the morning hours difficult.

To ensure the children's safety and smooth classroom function during arrival routines, use the following best practices:

- At the end of each workday, leave the classroom ready for the next morning. Prepare as many activities and materials as possible in advance so you'll have little prep to do during the morning rush.

- Arrive a few minutes early for your shift so you can be prepared to start work on time. Allow time before your shift to put away your personal things and to gather your thoughts about your tasks for the day. At the start of your shift, you should be in the classroom ready to interact with children and families.

- Plan morning activities that do not require your constant attention. Although you must always supervise the children, some activities can be a bit more child-directed. For example, tabletop activities such as playdough, puzzles, and building blocks are better choices than a read-aloud story or a puppet show.

- Stand near the door or in a location that allows you to see children and family members as they enter the classroom while supervising the children who have already arrived. Greet each family as they arrive.

- Add each child's name to your attendance as the child arrives in the classroom. Keep your child count accurate at all times.

- Be prepared for some challenges with separation from parents, even among older preschool-age children. It's developmentally typical for children to cry, be sad, or even be angry when they separate from their families each day. Reactions to separation will vary among children and may vary from day to day based on a child's mood, energy level, or other factors. Separation upset usually lasts only a few minutes. You can minimize it if you are prepared to distract the child with an individual activity, such as a song or story, and to offer comfort until the child feels calm.

- Watch for indicators from family members that they have information to share or need a few minutes of your time. They may have some special directions for the day, medication to drop off, or other information to communicate. Some programs use a log or other communication tools to record information shared by families in the morning. Be familiar with the way your program handles this.

- Help children store their belongings in their lockers, cubbies, bins, or baskets. Check for medications or other materials that need to be out of the reach of children.

- Suggest play activities to help arriving children integrate into the activity of the classroom.

APPLY YOUR KNOWLEDGE

Meet with your Orientation Mentor to gather information about morning routines in your program. Answer the following questions:

1. At what time(s) do children typically arrive in the classroom where you will work?

_____

_____

_____

2. What time does your shift begin?

_____

_____

_____

3. How does your program collect information shared by families in the morning? How does your program share this information among staff members?

_____

_____

_____

4. Where do children store their belongings?

_____

_____

_____

Meals and Snacks

The number of meals and snacks served in your classroom will depend on your program's hours of operation. Half-day programs may serve only one meal or snack, while full-day programs often serve two meals and two snacks. Infants typically eat when they're hungry, on individual schedules. Infants commonly eat (either food or a bottle, depending on the infant's age) every few hours. Toddlers and preschoolers also eat every two to three hours but typically participate in scheduled group meals.

Meal and snack preparation can occur in various ways. In some programs, children bring meals and snacks from home. Other programs provide meals and snacks, typically prepared in the program's kitchen and served family-style to the children in their classrooms. A full explanation of menu planning and food preparation is beyond the scope of this guide. If you will be involved in preparing children's food, you will receive specialized training for this task so you can learn the many regulations regarding food handling.

Feeding Infants

Infants need a great deal of nutrition to fuel their growth and development. But the foods they can eat and digest are limited. Most pediatricians recommend that infants have breast milk or infant formula during the first year. Typically, age-appropriate solid foods (baby foods) are introduced around six months of age.

When you are feeding infants, follow these best practices:

- Wash your hands before preparing infant bottles. You do not have to wear gloves when preparing bottles.

- Begin preparing bottles when you notice signs of hunger, such as sucking noises, opening mouth, and waving arms. Do not wait for an infant to begin crying before preparing for feeding.

- Check carefully to be sure that you are preparing the correct breast milk or formula for the baby. Double-check labels and instructions before preparing and feeding. If a baby accidentally drinks breast milk or formula from another child's bottle, follow your program's procedure for notifying the child's family.

- Prepare formula following the manufacturer's instructions. Warm the formula or breast milk as directed by a child's family so you are consistent with home practices. Do not warm infant bottles in a microwave. A microwave heats liquid unevenly in a baby bottle. This uneven heating causes hot spots, which can burn a baby's mouth even if you shake the bottle. Warm only as much milk or formula as the infant typically drinks in one feeding. Once a child has started drinking from a bottle, you should not return it to the refrigerator for later use. Discard unused milk or formula at the end of the feeding.

- Avoid mixing cereals or other foods into infant formula or breast milk in bottles. Spoon-feed cereals and other foods.

- Hold the baby while feeding with a bottle. Never prop the bottle to drain into his mouth or leave infants unattended holding their own bottles. Feeding is a time for closeness and bonding.

- Hold the bottle tipped *slightly* upside down, making sure the nipple is filled with liquid. This helps minimize the amount of air the infant swallows.

- Stop feeding every ounce or two to gently burp the baby. Hold the baby upright and gently pat her on the back. This helps her expel air and minimizes stomach upset after feeding.

- When spoon-feeding baby foods, hold a baby who is not yet fully independent in sitting in an upright position or place him in an infant seat designed for feeding. The infant should be sitting upright, not reclining while eating. When the baby is able to sit securely (does not slump over or slide out of an upright seat), you can use a low-to-the-ground feeding chair with tray (sometimes called a "low chair" for its resemblance to a high chair).

- When you're feeding baby foods, start with a small portion scooped into a bowl or dish. Discard any unused served baby food. To avoid wasting baby food, do not feed the baby directly from the baby food jar.

- Check the temperature of any warmed foods before feeding them to the baby. Foods should be warm but not hot. Stir foods to minimize hot spots.

- When you're spoon-feeding, place a small amount of food on the spoon and gently place the spoon in the baby's mouth. Wait for her to swallow the food before offering more. A spoon designed for infant feeding will help you offer an appropriate morsel of food and will make it easier to place the food in her small mouth.

- Stop feeding the infant when he shows signs of fullness by stopping sucking, turning away from the bottle or spoon, or consistently spitting out breast milk, formula, or food. Do not keep feeding the infant simply to use up all the food, breast milk, or formula.

- When feeding is done, discard any unused milk, formula, or food, and clean and sterilize the bottle, spoon, or other dishes. Discard the contents of any bottle that has been out of the refrigerator for more than an hour.

- Return the baby to play or lay her in the crib on her back if she's sleepy.

PRACTICAL TIP: Handling Breast Milk

Breast milk is the best choice for infant food. Breast milk is perfectly designed to meet the nutritional needs of infants and provides protection from illness and disease. Caregivers can play an important part in supporting mothers who breast-feed and use child care programs for their infants. To support mothers, follow these best practices:

- Express your desire to support the mother's decision to breast-feed.

- Prepare space for frozen breast milk and plan ahead how you will label and store the milk. The oldest breast milk should always be used first. Create a system that helps you easily identify which milk to thaw first. Frozen breast milk can be stored in a freezer with a separate door (not a freezer compartment within a refrigerator) for three to six months.

- Thaw breast milk in the refrigerator whenever possible. When time does not allow slow thawing in the refrigerator, thaw frozen breast milk by running warm water over the container or by swirling it in a bowl of warm water. Never use a microwave to thaw or warm breast milk. Microwaving can not only create hot spots, but it can also destroy the milk's special nutrients.

- Breast milk may separate. Swirl or gently shake the container to mix the milk. The color of breast milk varies based on the mother's diet. This is normal and presents no danger to the baby.

- You do not have to wear gloves when preparing or feeding breast milk. You should wash your hands before preparing bottles of breast milk or formula.

Toddler and Preschooler Meals and Snacks

Mealtimes and snacktimes present two important opportunities. First, they are a chance to support healthy development with nutritious food. Young children are growing quickly and using a great deal of energy in their everyday activities. They need nutritious foods to fuel their activities and their growth. Meals and snacks also offer opportunities to support children's social and emotional development through pleasant interactions and routines. When children eat together in small groups, they converse, share and take turns, and exercise their independence. Incorporate the following best practices into each day's mealtimes and snacktimes:

- Clean and sanitize tables and food-service surfaces (counters and so on) before food preparation begins.

- Involve children (as they are able) in helping prepare for meals and snacks. Children can set tables, pass out utensils, and so forth. Children and adults should thoroughly wash their hands before beginning preparations for meals or snacks.

- Do not gather children until you are ready for meals or snacks to begin. Organize food and utensils beforehand. Avoid asking the children to wait long periods of time for food to be served. If waiting for more than one or two minutes is unavoidable, engage the children in a song or story to fill the time.

- Be aware of children's food allergies, health-related food restrictions, and family food preferences. You must respect the families' preferences and dietary restrictions as long as they do not present a health hazard to young children.

- Before passing bowls or platters of food among the children, check the food for potential choking hazards and be sure that the utensils for serving are appropriate for the children's age and ability.

- Whenever possible, use family-style meal service to encourage children's independence and social development.

- Never use food as a punishment or reward. All children should have access to all foods, and foods should be served as a communal activity. Requiring children to clean their plate or to try a bite of certain foods before they can have fruits, desserts, or beverages is inappropriate.

- If children bring their own meals or snacks, circulate around the group and offer help with difficult packaging or storage containers. Model the technique for opening packages and encourage children to do as much as they can for themselves.

- During mealtimes or snacktimes, sit with the children and, if your program permits, eat with the children. This practice lets you model appropriate eating behaviors and pleasant social interactions. As you eat, discuss with the children the day's events

PRACTICAL TIP: Beverages

Beverages can either contribute to a healthy diet or pose a barrier to healthy eating. It's important to ensure that children's beverages are not empty calories. The following guidelines can help you promote a healthy diet and ensure children get the fluids they need each day for growth and development:

- Unflavored and fluoridated water should be accessible at all times to children over twelve months old. When children are thirsty, the first choice for a beverage should be water.

- All juices served should be 100 percent fruit juice with no added sweeteners or sugar. Juice should be limited to one four- to six-ounce serving per day.

- When you serve milk, it should be unflavored milk. After children wean from bottles, they should drink unflavored whole milk until twenty-four months of age. After twenty-four months, children should drink unflavored lowfat or nonfat milk.

or other interests of the group. Create a pleasant, relaxed atmosphere. Avoid rushing meals.

- Never force children to eat. Encourage children to try a variety of foods and model healthy variety in what you eat. Do not require children to eat all their food or to eat any food they dislike.

- Expect some spills. Have cleaning supplies nearby and engage children in age-appropriate cleanup tasks.

- Encourage children to stay seated while they eat. As children finish eating, you can direct them to clear their dishes, wash their hands, and join a play activity. Do not require all the children to remain at the table until everyone is finished.

- After all the children are finished eating, clean and sanitize the tables and food-service surfaces.

PRACTICAL TIP: Family-Style Meal Service

Many programs that prepare food on-site use a practice known as family-style meal service. They serve foods on platters or in bowls at the table, and they encourage children to serve themselves. This practice is similar to the way many families eat meals. It promotes social, emotional, and motor skills development. During a family-style meal, adults sit alongside children and encourage independence and self-help skills, while also promoting conversation and building relationships.

During meals served family-style, you are responsible for helping children who may need assistance and for observing carefully to be sure children get enough to eat and do not get frustrated with food-service tasks that are too difficult for their emerging skills. The following practices will help you make family-style meals pleasant learning opportunities for the children in your classroom:

- Arrange tables to facilitate small groups. Children function better in small groups of four to eight than in one large group. Whenever possible, position one adult at each table of children.

- Serve small bowls or platters of foods at each table. Supply appropriate-size utensils, such as tongs, scoops, and ladles, to encourage children to start with small portions and get second helpings as needed.

- Serve drinks from small pitchers so children can pour their own drinks into cups.

- When all the children at the table are seated, begin passing foods. Encourage children to start with a small portion of each food item. Reassure children that second helpings will be available if they are still hungry.

- Take your time and engage children in pleasant mealtime conversation. Eating should be a fun, social experience for children.

APPLY YOUR KNOWLEDGE

Meet with your Orientation Mentor to gather information about the way your program handles meals and snacks. Answer the following questions and complete the tasks described:

1. Which meals and snacks are served in your program? At what times do they happen?

   _____

2. How does your program serve meals (family-style or served by teachers)?

   _____

3. Who provides food for meals and snacks—families or the program's kitchen?

   _____

4. Where does your program store food-service supplies (plates, bowls, serving spoons, and so on)?

   _____

5. Observe and assist your Orientation Mentor before, during, and just after a meal and a snack in your assigned classroom.

   Initials _____

6. If you will work in an infant classroom, observe and assist your Orientation Mentor in labeling and storing infant bottles and foods. Observe procedures for handling breast milk and formula.

   Initials _____

7. If you will work in an infant classroom, observe and assist your Orientation Mentor in preparing infant bottles and foods and in bottle-feeding and spoon-feeding an infant. Observe procedures for handling breast milk and formula.

   Initials _____

8. How does your program inform parents of support for breast-feeding and procedures for storage and preparation of breast milk?

   _____

Diapering and Toileting

Elimination of body waste is a natural part of life. As an adult, you probably don't spend much time thinking about your need to use the bathroom or how you'll meet your needs. Because young children are just learning to control their elimination and to be independent in toileting, adults who care for them must put some thought into how they will handle children's elimination needs.

Most infants and toddlers use diapers and require diaper changing throughout the day. Many older toddlers are just starting to recognize their need for a diaper change or are becoming interested in using the toilet. Preschoolers are often just learning to use the toilet independently. They are still developing their skill in recognizing when they need to use the toilet and accomplishing the task.

You likely don't look forward to this aspect of working with young children. Few people would say that they enjoy diapering or helping children use the toilet. Regardless of how you feel, it is essential that you have a positive attitude about this responsibility and that you take advantage of daily diapering and toileting routines to support children's growing independence as well as their physical, social, and emotional health. Children can sense your feelings about your interactions with them and the jobs you are doing. When you're diapering children, you want them to feel secure and loved, not tolerated or rejected. The same goes for helping children who are learning to use the toilet. Using the toilet independently is a major milestone for young children. It signals to them that they are capable and growing up. Helping children master this challenging task requires patience and a positive attitude—even when the inevitable accidents happen.

Diapering

Most infants and toddlers wear diapers and lack sufficient physical control for learning to use the toilet. When you work with children in infant or toddler classrooms, diapering of children throughout the day will be among your assigned duties.

You should change children's diapers promptly whenever they are wet or soiled. And you will need to check each child at least every one to two hours to identify the need for diaper changing. You can also watch for signs that a child may be wet or soiled between checks. Children with wet or soiled diapers may cry, wiggle, pull at their diapers, or show no signs at all.

Diapering Procedure

You must handle diapering carefully to protect the child's health and safety as well as your health and the health of the other children in the group. Body waste can transmit germs that cause illness and infection. In addition to protecting health and safety, you must also diaper in a way that supports the child's social and emotional development. One-to-one interactions during diapering offer a good opportunity to establish warm, trusting relationships and to promote language and other cognitive skills.

Your program should have its diapering procedure posted in each diapering area. The posted procedure is designed to remind you to follow each step carefully each time you diaper a child. The best practices for diapering that follow are recommended by *Caring for Our Children: National Health and Safety Performance Standards; Guidelines for Early Care and Education Programs, Third Edition* (AAP, APHA, and NRC 2011):

1. Wash your hands.
2. Gather supplies and bring them to the diaper-changing area.
3. The diapering area should be clean, but if needed, clean and sanitize the area.
4. Bring the child to the diapering area. Hold the child away from your body slightly if the child's clothes are wet or soiled. If you are using gloves, put them on before handling soiled clothes or diapers.
5. Lay the child on the diaper-changing table. Keep at least one hand on the child at all times throughout the diapering procedure.
6. Remove the child's clothes so you can access the diaper. Minimize contact with soiled areas.
7. Unfasten the diaper, gently lift the child's legs, and clean the diapered area with disposable wipes. Remove feces and urine front to back, using a clean wipe each time you swipe. Put the soiled wipes into the soiled diaper, roll inward into a ball, and discard in a hands-free covered trash can.
8. Place any soiled clothes in a plastic bag to be taken home.
9. If you are using gloves, remove them now using proper technique to avoid contaminating hands. Place gloves in trash can.

10. Clean your hands and the child's hands with wipes. Discard wipes in trash can.

11. Put on a clean diaper and dress the child. Fasten the diaper carefully so it is not too tight (causing pinching) or too loose (causing leaking).

12. Wash the child's hands and gently return the child to a supervised play area.

13. Clean and disinfect the changing area and put away supplies.

14. Thoroughly wash your own hands.

15. Record diaper-changing information.

 **APPLY YOUR KNOWLEDGE**

Meet with your Orientation Mentor to gather information about the way in which your program handles diapering. Answer the following questions and complete the tasks described:

1. In which classrooms does diapering occur?

   _____

2. Who supplies diapers and diapering supplies? Where are they stored?

   _____

3. Where is the diapering procedure posted?

   _____

4. How is diaper-changing information recorded, and how is it shared with families?

   _____

5. Observe your Orientation Mentor conducting a diaper change.

   Initials _____

6. Conduct a diaper change while your Orientation Mentor observes you.

   Initials _____

Toileting

Most preschoolers use the bathroom somewhat independently, although a few may still be working on toilet learning. This does not mean that you have no responsibilities for helping preschoolers with elimination. They still need some support in this important task.

Apply the following best practices to the important task of supervising children's use of the bathroom:

- Ideally, bathroom facilities are accessible to the children throughout the day, and children are encouraged to use the toilet as needed. Scheduled toilet times are difficult for young children to follow. Also, scheduled toileting interferes with recognizing and responding to their bodies' elimination cues.

- From time to time, remind children to use the bathroom, and watch for signs that a child may need to use the toilet. Young children get distracted easily by play activities and forget to heed their bodies' elimination signals.

- Use praise and encouragement when prompting children to use the toilet. Never punish, tease, shame, humiliate, or threaten a child for toileting lapses.

- Supervise children when they are using the bathroom. Stand near the area and make sure children follow the rules for bathroom use.

- Children should use the bathroom one at a time. This prevents spreading of germs and inappropriate play.

- Remind children to use good hygiene, including wiping and hand washing after toileting. Help children as needed to be sure they return to play clean.

- Check the bathroom area frequently for spills, debris, and other messes that may need attention.

- Wash your hands thoroughly after helping any child in the bathroom or after cleaning up bathroom spills or messes.

Sometimes you will want all the children to use the bathroom. For example, all children should use the bathroom before naptime and before outdoor play. Several minutes before naptime or outdoor play begins, ask a child or two at a time to use the bathroom (depending on how many toilets are available). Avoid sending all the children to the bathroom area at once, as crowding and waiting can cause challenging behaviors.

APPLY YOUR KNOWLEDGE

Meet with your Orientation Mentor to gather information about the way in which your program handles toileting. Answer the following questions and complete the task described:

1. Where are the toilets used by children in your classroom?

_____

2. Where are toileting and hand-washing supplies stored?

_____

3. Where is the hand-washing procedure posted?

_____

4. How is toileting information recorded and how is it shared with families?

_____

5. What is the procedure for addressing toileting accidents?

_____

6. Observe and help your Orientation Mentor in supervising children during toileting.

Initials _____

Toilet Learning

Sometime between two and three years old, children begin to show interest in using the toilet. The ability to be potty trained, or use the toilet, depends on several developmental skills. For example, children need the physical development required for bladder and bowel control. They also need the fine-motor skills necessary for undressing and dressing to use the toilet and the cognitive skills that link the act of elimination with feelings of wetness or discomfort. And they must have the verbal skills to alert you to their need to be changed or to use the toilet.

Rushing to accomplish toilet learning before a child is developmentally ready seldom results in a good experience for you or the child. Working cooperatively with families to recognize signs of readiness is the best approach. Here are the typical signs of readiness:

- The child stays dry for long periods of time.
- The child alerts you when he is wet or soiled.
- The child expresses or demonstrates interest in using the toilet.
- The child is able to take clothes off and put them on before and after diaper changing.

Once you and a child's family have agreed to begin toilet learning, expect both progress and setbacks. You will need to be consistent and patient. The following best practices will help in toilet learning:

- Ask the family to supply several sets of extra clothes in case of accidents.
- Ask the family to dress the child in easy-to-remove clothes.
- Ask the child regularly to use the toilet. Reminders every two to three hours are a good idea.
- Watch for signs that a child may need to use the toilet, such as wiggling, nervousness, and so on. When you see these signs, gently direct the child to the bathroom.
- Expect accidents and setbacks as a normal part of the learning process. Never shame, humiliate, punish, or tease a child for a toileting lapse.
- Acknowledge successes and encourage the child along the way.

Outdoor Play

Children need daily opportunities for outdoor play whenever the weather and air quality do not pose safety risks. Outdoor play gives children the opportunity to practice physical skills such as running, jumping, and climbing. They engage in social activity and develop self-help skills along with growing confidence in their abilities. Children may also practice important cognitive skills when they solve problems and interact with outdoor play materials. And outdoor play provides time for children to connect with nature and learn in a different environment.

While outdoor play benefits young children's development in all domains, it also carries risks that you must manage. Adopt the following best practices when you're planning and doing outdoor play activities:

- Children should have an extended block of time each morning and afternoon for outdoor play. The amount of time spent outdoors will depend on the weather and the availability of indoor gross-motor activity.

- Adverse weather conditions should limit outdoor play. Adjust the length of outdoor play during cold or hot weather. For example, in hot weather, outdoor play may need to happen earlier in the day and be shortened. In some climates, children are prepared for outdoor play in cold weather. In climates where cold weather is uncommon, children may not have appropriate clothes for outdoor play.

- Skip outdoor play when the National Weather Service reports a windchill temperature of minus fifteen degrees or more Fahrenheit or a heat index at or over ninety degrees Fahrenheit. Also skip outdoor play when air quality is unhealthy.

- Encourage children to keep hydrated during outdoor play, especially in warm weather. Access to drinking water during outdoor play is important.

- Ensure that children are dressed for the weather. Work cooperatively with families to see that children have layers of clothing appropriate to the season, including hats and gloves. Avoid using long scarves or hats or hoods with dangling strings, as these can be a strangulation hazard during active play.

- Children are more prone to heat-induced illness and cold injuries than adults are. Check regularly to make sure children are not too cold or overheated.

- Avoid overexposure to the sun. Use the following sun-safety practices:

  - Infants younger than six months should stay out of direct sunlight. Use only shaded areas for infant outdoor play.
  - Encourage children to wear hats with wide brims to shade their faces during outdoor play.
  - Limit outdoor play during the hours of greatest sun exposure: 10:00 a.m. to 2:00 p.m.
  - Encourage children to wear sunglasses with ultraviolet (UV) protection.
  - Apply sunscreen with a sun protection factor (SPF) of fifteen or higher thirty minutes before outdoor play. Reapply every two hours if children will be outside for extended periods of time.

- Conduct regular attendance and child counts. When you're moving groups of children to the outdoor play yard and back inside, take attendance to be sure you've accounted for everyone in your care. Take regular attendance during outdoor playtime to guarantee ongoing supervision.

- Supervise outdoor play closely. Many childhood injuries occur during outdoor play because children may not fully understand the risks of some play behaviors or may overestimate their physical abilities. Outdoor playtime is not a time to gather with colleagues for conversation or to relax your active supervision.

- Identify areas of the outdoor play yard that present the greatest risks to children. Here are the areas that commonly present challenges to supervision:

  - ladders and steps
  - bottoms of slides

- ‣ bodies of water
- ‣ area around swings
- ‣ areas near sheds, gates, or doors

- Promote active play while children are outdoors. Lead children in games with running, jumping, and other vigorous exercise.

- Suggest activities to children who seem bored or uninvolved. Sometimes children have trouble starting play activities. Or children may have a hard time joining the play of others. Be prepared to offer suggestions or support children in starting or joining play activities.

- Rotate materials and equipment in the play yard from time to time. Keep outdoor play interesting by bringing out new activities, such as paint, sidewalk chalk, balls, hoops, parachutes, or mats. In warm weather, water play using spray bottles or a water table or tubs can also liven up the outdoor play.

- Sweep sand routinely from sidewalks during outdoor play to prevent slips and falls.

- Just before the end of outdoor playtime, involve the children in cleaning up the play yard. Park bikes and tricycles and put away balls, sand toys, and other loose equipment. Leave the play yard tidy and ready for the next group of children.

- When children return to the classroom, remind them to wash their hands. Quickly take attendance to make sure everyone has returned to the classroom.

PRACTICAL TIP: Windchill

Windchill is the temperature that it feels like outside considering the effects of wind and cold on the skin. When wind speed increases, the body cools faster, and it feels colder than the air temperature may indicate. Therefore, you must take into account the windchill when making decisions about the safety of outdoor play.

PRACTICAL TIP: Sunscreen and Insect Repellent

Sunscreen is often used to minimize children's exposure to the sun's harmful effects. Insect repellent can be applied to prevent bites from insects that may carry disease. Sunscreens and insect repellents are typically considered over-the-counter medications, and in most cases, their use requires family permission. Follow the instructions on the label. Read the directions carefully, and note the ages of children for whom the product is approved and the frequency with which the product must be applied.

PRACTICAL TIP: Water

Children love water play. But water play does present challenges. Even a very small amount of water can pose a danger to children, who can drown easily. Also, water can harbor disease-carrying insects and can be a breeding ground for germs. When you plan water play activities, use the following best practices:

- Always supervise children very closely around water. Children can never be alone in an area with a pool (even a child-size pool, such as a wading pool).
- Make sure that children do not drink the water used for water play.
- Use sprinklers, spray bottles, and other moving water whenever possible. This minimizes hazards (but does not minimize the need for supervision).
- Empty water tables, tubs of water, watering cans, and so on after each use. Clean and sanitize surfaces. Do not allow standing water in buckets, bins, or tubs overnight.
- Reapply sunscreen often during water play. Differing brands of sunscreen offer differing levels of water resistance; check the sunscreen label for recommendations.

APPLY YOUR KNOWLEDGE

Meet with your Orientation Mentor to gather information about the way in which your program handles outdoor play. Answer the following questions and complete the task described:

1. When is outdoor play typically scheduled for your classroom?

    _____

2. Where are outdoor play materials and equipment stored?

    _____

3. How should you track attendance of children during outdoor play?

    _____

4. What are your program's guidelines for inclement weather? Who makes the decision?

    _____

5. Observe and assist your Orientation Mentor in supervising children during outdoor play.

    Initials _____

Naptime Routines and Safe Sleep

Young children are very busy throughout the day exploring, playing, growing, and learning. All this activity is tiring for them. When children are tired, they have a hard time controlling their emotions and playing cooperatively. Like tired adults, tired children can be short-tempered, irritable, difficult to reason with, and hard to please. Naps serve an important developmental function. While sleeping, children rest their minds and muscles, recharging them for active play later in the day, and their brains get a chance to organize the information they have received.

Therefore, it is typical—and desirable—for children to rest for some part of the day. Infants may sleep for short periods several times a day. Toddlers may take morning and afternoon naps. Preschoolers often take just one nap a day in the early afternoon. The amount of sleep each child needs is unique, but most programs plan for about two hours of afternoon naptime for toddlers and preschoolers and a shorter morning nap for some or all toddlers.

Safe Sleep for Infants

Infants typically nap for short periods of time throughout the day, each infant on her own schedule. The amount, frequency, and duration of sleep will vary among the infants in your program. As infants age, their naps tend to get longer and less frequent. So by the end of the first year, children commonly take only a morning and an afternoon nap.

It is hard to imagine that sleep could be dangerous to infants. But you must follow some key practices to ensure that sleeping infants are also safe infants. You can minimize the risks of suffocation, entrapment, strangulation, and sudden infant death syndrome (SIDS) with the following precautions:

- All infants should sleep in a crib approved by the Consumer Product Safety Commission with a firm, fitted mattress. Sleeping in car seats, swings, infant seats, or any other place that is not an

Sudden Unexplained Infant Deaths

Each year approximately 3,500 infants in the United States die suddenly and unexpectedly (CDC 2015). These infants are not ill, and initially the cause of death may be unknown. After investigation, about one-half of these deaths are typically attributed to unsafe sleep practices and the resulting suffocations, strangulations, or entrapments. The remaining deaths often cannot be explained and are labeled as SIDS. CDC defines SIDS as "the sudden death of an infant less than one year of age that cannot be explained after a thorough investigation is conducted, including a complete autopsy, examination of the death scene, and a review of the clinical history" (CDC 2015). Because the exact cause of SIDS is unknown, it cannot be fully prevented. However, research has shown a relationship between safe sleep practices and a great decrease in SIDS deaths. Safe sleep practices can also prevent other causes of infant deaths during sleep, including strangulations, entrapments, and suffocations.

approved crib should be prohibited. If an infant falls asleep some-place other than a crib, gently move the infant to a crib as soon as possible.

- Infant cribs should be free of soft items such as bumper pads, pillows, cushions, bolsters, blankets, stuffed animals, and so on. These items are unnecessary, and they present a suffocation hazard.

- Place infants only on their backs to sleep unless a physician has directed you in writing to use an alternate sleep position. When infants are old enough to roll over on their own, it is fine to leave them in the positions they roll into—but always start sleep with the infant on his back.

- Cribs should be located away from windows, electrical outlets, and hanging decorations. Never string toys across a crib or use a pacifier on a string in a crib.

- Keep the infant area a comfortable temperature, neither cold nor hot. The area should be warm enough that blankets are not needed but not so warm that infants are flushed or sweating.

- Maintain supervision when infants are sleeping. Continue to keep a close watch on sleeping infants so that you will be able to notice a baby who is in any kind of distress. Sleeping infants should be visible and within hearing.

PRACTICAL TIP: Blanket Sleepers or Sleep Sacks

Eliminating blankets from infant cribs is the safest choice, but this can be hard for families to understand. They—and perhaps you—may fear that infants will get cold when they are not actively playing. Blanket sleepers and specially designed sleep sacks are safe alternatives to blankets. These clothes go on over an infant's play clothes but cannot cover the infant's face and cause suffocation.

Nap Guidelines and Routines

Like any important part of the day, naptime requires preparation and attention to best practices. Most infants, toddlers, and young preschoolers require sleep during the day. Older preschoolers may require less sleep, and some may only rest (but not fall asleep) for a brief period of time. It is important to plan for children who fall asleep easily, children who have difficulty falling asleep, and children who do not sleep at all. The following practices will help you have a safe, healthy, and calming naptime in your classroom:

- Each child should have her own cot, mat, or crib for naptime. Children should never use the same cot, crib, or mat at the same time. If the same one is used by different children on different days, you must clean and sanitize it between uses. Cribs, cots, or mats should be cleaned and sanitized weekly and when soiled.

- Children's bedding, crib sheets, cot sheets, and blankets must be cleaned at least weekly and when soiled. Children should never share bedding on different days unless it's cleaned between uses.

- Cribs and cots or mats should be placed at least three feet apart. Also, position children head-to-toe on cots or mats to minimize the spread of airborne illnesses. Many teachers develop a chart to show where each child's cot or mat is placed. This consistency may be helpful to some children.

- Supervise sleeping children of all ages. Children should be within sight and hearing at all times, even when sleeping or resting. Children's heads and faces should be uncovered. If a child covers his face, gently uncover it.

- Schedule naptimes for toddlers and preschoolers at predictable times each day. Follow a predictable routine before naptime. Use calming activities, such as a quiet story or music, to set the tone for rest. Gently remind children that they need to rest so that they will be ready for play later in the day. Use a calm and reassuring voice.

- Let children over one year old use a blanket, stuffed animal, or other item from home to help them relax and feel secure enough to drift off to sleep. Toddlers and some young preschoolers may still use a pacifier at naptime. Check with families to understand each child's typical sleep routines.

- Quietly circulate around the room, helping calm children who have a more difficult time transitioning to sleep. Offer to rub a child's back gently to help with restlessness.

- Prepare a few quiet activities for children who no longer nap. After a short rest (typically thirty minutes or so), some children may be ready to resume activity. Quiet activities away from the napping area could include puzzles, table toys, playdough, and the like. Do not require children to stay on their mats or cots for extended periods of time if they are not sleeping.

- As children wake from napping, gently direct them to the quiet play activities until most children are awake. When nearly all the children are awake, you can resume the day's activities. Whenever possible, let children wake from napping on their own.

PRACTICAL TIP: Lighting

It is essential that you keep supervising children while they are resting or sleeping. The room cannot be so dark that you cannot observe the children or safely move around the room. Many programs use dim lighting by installing dimmer switches or by switching off half of the lighting during naptime. Some programs also use small area lights, such as safe desk lamps, during naptime. When using area lights or lamps, be careful that cords do not cause a tripping hazard and that outlets are covered when not in use.

APPLY YOUR KNOWLEDGE

Meet with your Orientation Mentor to gather information about the way in which your program handles naptime. Answer the following questions and complete the tasks described:

1. What special naptime requirements, if any, must your program follow? This might include use of mats or cots, supervision, length of time spent napping, and so on.

   _____

   _____

   _____

2. What are the typical naptimes for the classroom where you will work?

   _____

   _____

   _____

3. Where are cots, mats, and bedding for naptime stored? Are they labeled?

   _____

   _____

   _____

4. What is the classroom staff:child ratio during naptime?

   _____

   _____

   _____

5. When are cots, mats, or cribs cleaned and sanitized? Who is responsible for this task?

_____

_____

_____

6. When is sleep bedding cleaned? Who is responsible for this task?

_____

_____

_____

7. Observe and assist in a transition to naptime in the classroom where you will work.

_____

_____

Initials _____

8. Observe and assist in a transition following naptime.

Initials _____

Learning Activities

Young children are always learning. Everything you do, or choose not to do, affects the learning of the children in your care. They see you as a role model, so your actions, words, interactions, and attitude help steer their development. In addition to the informal learning that occurs through interacting with children throughout the day, most teachers also plan learning activities for large and small groups of children.

Sometimes children's learning activities are hard to identify because they look like children are just playing. Actually, young children learn best when they are playing. Play is the way children experiment, explore, and try to understand the world around them. Through play, children try new things, test ideas, interact socially, act on their curiosity, and solve big and small problems. When children spend most of the day playing, they are actually spending most of the day learning.

Although play is the best way to encourage children's learning, that does not mean that play activities are unplanned or that you are not teaching throughout the day. Early childhood teachers are constantly planning and teaching. You are responsible for planning playful activities that help the young children in your care reach important developmental goals. You will select goals to work on, plan activities, arrange the environment, and interact with children to engage them in playful activities that present opportunities to develop and practice skills they will use as lifelong learners.

Program Goals, Curriculum, and Assessment

Most early childhood programs embrace the notion that young children need both care and education. While it is easy to describe the kind of care children need—supervision, feeding, changing, and so forth—it is harder to describe what education looks like in early childhood. Fortunately, most programs have a set of goals for children's development that guide teachers in crafting the learning activities, or curriculum, for the children. The program goals may be associated with a particular curriculum, an assessment tool, or a regulatory agency or other governing body. For example, your state may have established early learning guidelines, or standards that describe what young children should know and be able to do before kindergarten entry. These standards become the goals associated with early childhood programs. Many commercial curricula are based on learning goals for young children developed from years of research on children's development. These learning goals are often called objectives by curriculum publishers.

Regardless of whether they are called goals, standards, objectives, or something else, these statements will help you determine what activities to plan for your classroom. For example, if one of the learning objectives for the age group you are teaching states that children should be able to recognize and name numerals one to ten, you will likely be planning and implementing many fun, playful activities for the children to help them demonstrate this skill. Your

What Is Curriculum?

The term *curriculum* is often used in early childhood programs to refer to the planned learning activities carried out throughout the day. A high-quality curriculum is more than a few activities for group time. Rather, it provides a framework for supporting children's development through the arrangement of the environment, the materials selected for children's use, the interactions teachers have with children, and the planned learning activities that take place in large and small groups. Using a curriculum involves setting goals for children's learning and accomplishing those goals in developmentally appropriate ways. A curriculum for infants will look quite different from one for preschoolers because the children are able to do different things, they have different interests, and they are working on different developmental goals. All curricula for young children should involve them in hands-on, fun-filled, playful activity, as this is the way children learn best.

All early childhood curricula use developmentally appropriate practices. But this does not mean that all curricula are the same. Early childhood programs use varying philosophies and curriculum types. Some programs organize their curricula using weekly or monthly themes or topics. In these programs, teachers choose a theme or topic of study and plan activities that complement the theme. For example, a classroom's theme for one week might be "My Home," and activities might focus on types of homes, things in a child's home, and more. Other curricula use projects or investigations as a framework for learning activities. In programs using these curricula, children might participate in activities that help them investigate a topic, such as water, or answer a question, such as "How do plants grow?" Regardless of your program's curriculum type or philosophy, classroom activities must match the abilities and interests of the children to be truly effective.

program's curriculum may suggest activities that introduce this skill and provide practice opportunities for children. And you will have many opportunities to reinforce the children's emerging skill through your interactions with them as they play throughout the day.

Some programs use a commercially produced curriculum to aid in carrying out learning activities, while others count on their teachers to design and develop the plans for learning activities, often referred to as lesson plans. Regardless of whether your program uses a commercially produced curriculum or one of your own design, you may be responsible for some planning, and you will certainly be responsible for a great deal of the implementation of learning activities.

In addition to planning and carrying out learning activities, you may also be involved in assessing young children's learning. Assessment involves understanding and documenting which developmental goals or objectives children have met and determining next steps in your learning activities. The word *assessment* may remind you of tests or exams from your own educational experience. As you can imagine, giving a young child a test—especially a written one—isn't an accurate measure of what the child knows or can do. But young children do demonstrate every day through their play the many skills they're learning and have mastered. So in early childhood, assessment is usually a matter of observing young children while they play and learn.

Your program may use either a commercially produced assessment tool or a self-produced one. In some cases, you as the teacher may be responsible for determining how you will assess the children in your classroom. Regardless of which type of assessment you use, your careful observation of the children and your knowledge of their development will be critical to accurate assessment. And this information will be useful to you in planning your curriculum. The following graphic illustrates the relationship between curriculum and assessment.

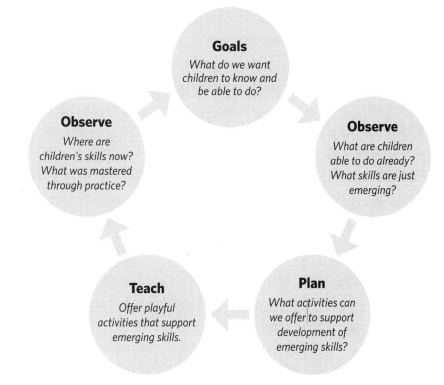

Notice that this process is cyclical. Teaching young children involves constantly setting goals, observing, planning and implementing playful activities, and then reassessing where children are in order to set new goals.

Group Activities

Most classrooms have time each day when all the children gather as a group. These whole-group activities are often called group time or circle time. Your classroom may also have times when children gather in small groups for learning activities. Group activities give children a chance to practice important social skills while they participate in songs, stories, group games, and the like. Group activities are also a time when community building happens. For example, you may use group time to acknowledge children's birthdays, to celebrate meeting class goals, or to conduct routines and rituals such as selecting classroom helpers, reminding children about classroom rules, or sharing news from home. When you're organizing and carrying out large- or small-group activities, keep the following principles in mind:

- **Vary your plan with children's ages and abilities.** Infants rarely have whole-group activities because babies follow their own schedules of eating, sleeping, and playing. But when a few infants are awake and interested, you might gather a small group for a song or short story. Toddlers and preschoolers typically have one or two short whole-group times each day and may also have one or two small-group activities throughout the day. The younger the children, the shorter the group time should be, because young children are just learning to regulate their behavior and to focus on one task for a period of time. For example, a typical group time for toddlers might be only ten to fifteen minutes long, while a group time for preschoolers might be fifteen to twenty minutes—or longer, in some cases.

- **Keep it short and active.** Young children are active learners who have not yet developed the ability to focus their attention on one activity for long periods of time. A ten-minute group time is rarely one long activity. Rather, it usually consists of two or three activities that last only a couple of minutes each. For example, it might include a short song, an action rhyme or fingerplay, and a movement activity such as acting out the song "I'm a Little Teapot."

- **Plan and prepare in advance.** When you gather children for group times, you must be prepared to start right away. Young children will not wait patiently while you gather supplies, get organized, review your notes, and so on. Do any preparation required before you bring children to the group. Children are attracted to fun, playful activities, so use a song or other appealing activity as a way to gather the children in the group. When you begin, they will join you.

- **Be flexible about attendance and participation.** Some children will naturally join the group right away, participate in every activity, and beg for more when group time is over. Other children may be more reluctant to join the group or may prefer to observe rather than join in. Some children may wander in and out of group time. This behavior is typical for young children—especially toddlers or children who are new to group experiences. Be patient and flexible. You can encourage children to join in, but do not focus your attention on one child's reluctance at the expense of the whole group's activity. Put your effort into making your group times interesting and fun. Eventually this will attract even the most reluctant child.

- **Combine familiar activities with new ones.** Children love repetition, and repeating familiar favorites not only helps children feel secure but also reinforces their learning. At the same time, new activities stretch children's skills and keep them interested in group time. As you plan your large and small groups, strive for a combination of familiar activities such as songs, stories, and games with new activities that focus on children's interests and emerging skills.

- **Use group size wisely.** Some activities work well in whole groups; others work best in smaller groups of three to five children. For example, it is no fun for a group of twenty preschoolers to play a board game. It takes too long for each child's turn to come around, and children quickly lose interest. But a simple board game may be a perfect small-group activity; it offers an opportunity to build skills such as counting, problem solving, and so on, while practicing important social skills such as turn taking. As you select activities that match the learning objectives of your program, think carefully about the best teaching method and group size for each activity.

- **Be prepared to adjust your plan.** Even the best plan occasionally needs adjustment. Despite your best efforts to select activities that match children's abilities and interests, some activities may not engage the children or may not turn out as you expect. When children lose interest, appear bored, or exhibit challenging behaviors, it is time to make an adjustment. You can quickly switch to a new activity, add something active, or conclude the group time and move on to something else. Do not hesitate to try your plan again later in the day or another day.

Most teachers put considerable time into planning large- and small-group activities for the children in their classroom. This planning time is time well spent. But group time is not the only aspect of the curriculum that requires thoughtful planning.

Room Arrangement and Equipment

An important aspect of planning your classroom curriculum is selecting equipment and arranging the furniture. Like adults, children are influenced by their environment. Materials that are safe, clean, easy to find and put away, and interesting to the children encourage their growing independence. Conversely, when materials are hard to find, stored haphazardly, too few in number, or frustrating or uninteresting to the children, challenging behaviors are likely to result.

The classroom where you will work probably already has furniture and equipment. You may have an opportunity over time to request additional supplies, and you probably have some flexibility in how you use the materials that are already on hand. The following principles should guide your use of space and equipment:

- **Put safety first.** No toy or piece of furniture has developmental value if it is dangerous. As sensorimotor learners, children must be able to touch and explore equipment in the early childhood classroom. Check for and eliminate toys or furniture with the following hazards:

▸ sharp edges

▸ broken or cracked pieces or pieces with peeling paint

▸ small, chokable pieces (Anything small enough to fit through a cardboard toilet-paper tube is too small for infants and toddlers, who are likely to mouth toys.)

▸ dirty toys or equipment (Clean them before using.)

▸ long strings, pull cords, or ropes that can cause strangulation

▸ toxic materials such as glues, some paints, and so on (Check labels to ensure supplies are nontoxic.)

● **Match equipment to the children's ages and abilities.** The right equipment for an infant classroom would not be a good fit in a preschool classroom. Toys and equipment must be safe and interesting for the children. To be interesting, toys and equipment must be at the right level of challenge—not so difficult as to be frustrating, but not so easy that they are quickly mastered without effort. Start with the manufacturer recommendations for user ages and adjust your offerings based on your observations of the children.

● **Have sufficient quantities available.** Young children are just learning to share and take turns. Having too few toys available exacerbates disputes over materials and does not help children learn social skills. When enough toys and materials are on hand, including duplicates of some popular toys, children learn that they will have access to many things to do and that they need not fight over toys.

● **Plan for variety in toys and equipment.** In addition to having enough toys, you must have a variety of toys. Children have varying interests, and individual children will not be interested in the same toys day after day. To support well-rounded development, you need to have a variety of toys that address many skills and interests. For example, a well-rounded classroom has building blocks, art materials, books, games, dramatic play (dress-up and housekeeping) materials, climbing toys, push and pull toys, small manipulative toys (such as pegboards and interlocking blocks like Legos), and more. Some teachers are fortunate to have a large supply of materials that can be rotated in and out of the classroom to increase variety and spark interest.

- **Neatly arrange toys and materials in logical and predictable locations.** Arranging toys and materials where they are easily accessible supports children's growing independence. When children can find what they need and replace it when they are done, they feel confident and capable. Also, when children are more self-directed, you focus more on scaffolding children's learning and less on finding and cleaning up toys.

- **Adjust the environment over time.** Children's needs and interests change over time, and you must adjust the environment in response. For example, you may find that the children in your class love block play, but the block area in your classroom is small and quickly becomes crowded with children and their structures. You may need to increase the size of this area to accommodate its growing popularity. If, over time, the children's interest in block play wanes, you can always return the block area to its original size.

PRACTICAL TIP: Learning Centers

Early childhood classrooms are often arranged into learning centers or interest areas. Teachers use furnishings such as shelves or tables to create areas where specific types of toys and equipment are stored. For example, your classroom may have a block center, an art center, a library or book center, and many more. Learning centers help children predict where they will find certain toys and materials. And, because related toys and materials are arranged together, children's play is often richer and more interesting. Learning centers also help children naturally form small groups for play, which supports their growing social skills. Throughout the day, children need long blocks of time to freely explore the many learning centers within the classroom. This gives them the opportunity to experience variety and to practice a wide range of skills.

Transitions

Throughout the day, children move from activity to activity. Sometimes this change in activity also involves a change in location, such as going from indoors to outdoors. That time between activities or places is called a transition. Transitions can be difficult for young children because they are naturally focused on their own needs and wants, and they are not yet skilled at following directions. For example, imagine you are a toddler and have just started working on a building in the block center. Your teacher tells you it is time to clean up and have lunch. Your natural tendency is to keep doing what you're already doing—building with blocks—and resist changing activities. And, because you have limited understanding of consequences, it might not occur to you that missing lunch would be very unpleasant.

One of your important goals as a teacher of young children is to help them learn to regulate their own behavior, including moving between activities. Helping children master this skill not only supports their development but prevents many challenging behaviors that often occur during transitions and thereby makes the day go more smoothly. The following guidelines will help you navigate transitions in a way that supports children's emerging skills:

- **Minimize the number of transitions throughout the day.** Although children change activities frequently, it is wise to minimize the number of times *you* are asking them to change spaces, groups, and activities. Plan for long blocks of time in the morning and afternoon during which children can move freely from one activity to the next or from one group of playmates to another.

- **Plan for transitions by using predictable routines.** Children perform best when they know what you expect of them. Creating predictable routines for transitions helps children anticipate what will happen and recall the expected behavior. For example, when you sing the same song each time cleanup is needed, children learn that the song is a signal for a certain kind of behavior. Plan predictable routines for the transitions that occur each day, such as going outside, cleaning up, going to meals or snacks, and settling in for naptime.

- **Give warnings before transitions take place.** Let children know what's coming a few minutes before transitions. For example, say,

"We will be cleaning up very soon, so finish what you are working on." These warnings give children a chance to prepare for the upcoming change of activity or space.

- **Give clear one- or two-step directions.** When you're directing children in transitions, give directions one or two steps at a time. Children have short memories and focus only on the task they need to do right now. They are likely to forget the last few steps of a long list of directions. For example, tell the children, "Put the blocks on the shelf, then go to the sink to wash your hands." Once the children have completed these steps, give the next direction.

- **Keep it fun and active.** Transitions can be difficult but do not have to be the worst parts of your day. Since transitions happen often, it is important to incorporate them into your plan for the children's playful learning. Use transitions as time to sing a song, play a guessing game, or conduct a movement activity. For example, when you're moving from the classroom to the playground, ask the children to walk like an elephant or hop like a bunny. These games keep children focused on the task, make the transitions fun parts of the day, and provide opportunities to incorporate some additional learning, too.

APPLY YOUR KNOWLEDGE

Meet with your Orientation Mentor to gather information about the way your program plans and carries out learning activities. Answer the following questions and complete the tasks described:

1. What learning goals, standards, or objectives does your program use?

_____

_____

_____

_____

2. What curriculum does your program use?

_____

_____

_____

_____

3. What type of lesson plans does your program use? Who develops the lesson plans? Are lesson plans approved? If so, when and by whom?

_____

_____

_____

_____

4. Does your program use themes to organize learning activities? If so, who chooses the themes?

_____

_____

_____

_____

5. When and how often does your classroom conduct group activities? Who decides the length and schedule for group activities? Who selects the activities?

_____

_____

_____

_____

6. What resources are available to support curriculum planning? Where are these resources located?

_____

_____

_____

7. What assessment tools does your program use? What are the expectations for observation and assessment of the children?

_____

_____

_____

8. What are the rules for arranging classroom furnishings? Who decides when to move or replace furnishings?

_____

_____

_____

9. What materials are available for use in classroom activities? Where are materials stored? How are new materials requested?

_____

_____

_____

10. Take a short tour with your Orientation Mentor of the curriculum and assessment materials used in your program. Look at any manuals, forms, checklists, or other resources that are available to you—whether they are required or simply suggested.

    Initials _____

11. Take another tour with your Orientation Mentor of the classroom where you will work. Note the furniture and equipment available in the room as well as the current room arrangement and learning centers.

    Initials _____

12. Take a tour with your Orientation Mentor of the supplies available for use in the classroom. Visit any supply closets, storerooms, or other locations where supplies are routinely stored.

    Initials _____

13. Observe and help your Orientation Mentor in conducting a transition between activities.

    Initials _____

14. Conduct a transition between activities while your Orientation Mentor observes your techniques.

    Initials _____

Communicating with Families

Your day will include not only work with children but also contact with the families of those children. During the early years, family members are very interested in their children's progress in your program. They are interested in their child's daily care routines—eating, sleeping, and toileting—and how the child is growing and developing. Fortunately, you'll have many opportunities each day to communicate with families, both informally and formally.

Informal Communication

Each day during arrival and departure, you'll have opportunities to talk informally with families. These casual conversations present a chance to get to know one another, to build partnerships, and to share information about the children. You can take full advantage of these informal conversations by following these guidelines:

- **Focus on the positive.** Arrival and departure are not the times for heavy, complex conversations. First, your attention is divided between conversing and supervising the children. And second, family members are not prepared for difficult conversations during these times. They may be on a tight schedule or may not be emotionally ready to hear something difficult. When you anticipate a difficult conversation, schedule a time to meet with the family.

- **Open the conversation and be prepared to listen.** It is up to you, as the professional in the classroom, to greet families and start conversations. Conversation starters such as "How was your day?" are fine for this purpose. Once the conversation gets going, be prepared to listen, not just talk. Remember, a conversation is two-way communication.

- **Avoid listing all the day's challenges.** You will have already addressed most challenging behaviors through your active guidance. Unless you are working together on a specific challenge, family members do not need to hear every detail of their children's behavior. Instead, focus on the day's overall successes.

- **Remember professionalism, ethics, and confidentiality.** As you get to know families better and better, you might find it more difficult to maintain professional boundaries and to keep information confidential. Family members begin to know you and other children, and they may sense challenges or frustrations you are having with a child's behavior, program policies, personal issues, or coworkers. Despite this familiarity, it is appropriate to share with families only information about their own children.

In addition to casual or informal conversations, you may have more formal communications with families during the day that help you share information about their children's growth and development.

Formal Communications

Most programs have several modes of formal communication with families. Your program may have a website, a family handbook, bulletin boards, a social media page, or newsletters that convey information to enrolled and prospective families. Some programs also have a written or electronic method for communicating with each family during or at the end of the day. This communication may include information about what the child ate, how the child slept, diapering or toileting, and learning activities. Some programs send pictures and instant messages to families to keep them up to date with the children's day. Even though this kind of communication is easy and fast, it still requires care on your part. When you communicate with families in writing, remember the following guidelines:

- **Neatness, spelling, and grammar matter.** Your writing is a reflection of your professionalism and of your program's quality. Families expect that you will model high-quality writing. Before you hand out a note or hit "send" on an electronic communication, take a moment to check spelling and proofread everything you have written.

- **Choose your topics wisely.** Some information is perfect for a note or an e-mail; other information needs to be conveyed in person—either over the phone or face-to-face. A good rule of thumb is to put yourself in the family member's shoes. Would you want to hear this information in person? Or would you want to receive it via a note or an e-mail?

- **Follow rules of confidentiality, ethics, and professionalism.** Whether your communication is spoken or written, the same rules apply. Remember, inappropriate information in written form is even easier to pass along than in spoken form. Assume any e-mail you send could be forwarded to any number of other people. How would you feel if that happened?

- **Slow down and check your facts.** Before you put anything in writing, be sure you have the facts straight. One handy aspect of written communication is that it gives you a chance to plan what you are going to say and get the message just right. Take advantage of this to make sure your message is well crafted and accurate. Enlist the help of an experienced colleague or your director when you are unsure how to explain something or whether your message is clear and on point.

- **Use the resources available to you.** Many programs have well-established forms, form letters, or other communication tools from which you can draw. Take advantage of these tools to save time and to benefit from your colleagues' experience in communicating with families.

APPLY YOUR KNOWLEDGE

Meet with your Orientation Mentor to gather information about the way your program handles communication with families. Answer the following questions and complete the task described:

1. How does your program share daily information about eating, sleeping, diapering, toileting, and learning? What forms or formats are used? Who completes this information?

   _____

   _____

   _____

   _____

   _____

2. What other communication tools does the program use? What responsibilities do teachers have for newsletters, bulletin boards, and so on?

   _____

   _____

   _____

   _____

   _____

3. Does your program use electronic communication? If so, when? Who communicates electronically?

_____

_____

_____

_____

_____

4. Take a tour with your Orientation Mentor of your program's communication tools. Look at bulletin boards, past newsletters, forms used for daily communication, and so forth.

   Initials _____

Departure Routines

At the end of each program day, children leave to go home with their families. Different programs organize departures differently. In some programs, all the children leave at the same time. In other programs, children leave at varying times throughout the day. Fortunately, the times when children depart each day are typically fairly consistent and predictable.

Following are some things to be aware of as children depart from the program each day:

- Ask the center director for information about any children who have specific custody arrangements defining who may pick up the children and when. This will help you make sure that only authorized adults pick up the children.

- Each day, check with your director and colleagues about changes to a child's typical pickup routine. You should be aware if a child is leaving early, staying later than usual, or being picked up by someone other than usual.

- Stand near the door or in a location where you can observe families arriving for pickup while supervising the children who remain in the classroom. This will help you monitor children's departures and make it easier to converse with family members. Remember to balance your desire to communicate with families with your responsibility for supervising the children in your care.

- Plan activities for the children that allow them to be fairly independent. Activities similar to those planned for arrival times are also good choices for departure times.

- Greet family members when they arrive to pick up children. Be prepared to tell them a few things their children did during the day and how the day progressed.

- Keep an accurate count of the number of children in your care. As children depart with their families, adjust your attendance so that you are sure at a moment's notice how many children, and which children, you are responsible for.

- Be alert to who is picking up each child. In most cases, one of a child's parents will be picking up the child. You must be prepared to ask for identification if a person unknown to you attempts to pick up a child. You must also verify with the director that this person has approval to pick up the child.

- After all children have departed for the day, conduct your normal cleanup and closing routines.

APPLY YOUR KNOWLEDGE

Meet with your Orientation Mentor to gather information about the way your program handles daily departures. Answer the following questions and complete the task described:

1. Do the children in your classroom have any special custody or pickup arrangements?

   _____

   _____

   _____

   _____

2. How are changes to children's typical pickup routines communicated?

   _____

   _____

   _____

   _____

3. How should you track changes in attendance as children depart?

   _____

   _____

   _____

   _____

4. Observe and assist your Orientation Mentor during your program's departure time.

   Initials _____

Team Communication

Most programs rely on a team of people to provide the children's care and education. As a member of a team, you have responsibilities both to the children and to the team. Teams function best when communication is frequent, thorough, and solution-oriented. Team communication is easy when things are going well and the messages are the simple details of daily activities, but more challenging when things are not going well or when conflicts erupt. Even well-functioning teams made up of members with good intentions occasionally have conflicts about the best course of action. This is to be expected when people care passionately about their work and when the outcomes of that work are so important. In fact, conflicts, when handled professionally, can help teams find creative solutions and improve their overall level of service to children and families. The following guidelines will help you communicate effectively with your colleagues and team members:

- **Communicate frequently.** Never assume that your colleagues already know everything they need to know. For example, when a family member shares information about a child's early departure, share that information right away with any team members who may be present later in the day. Do not assume that the family member has told others in the program.

- **Use established communication tools.** Most programs have specific ways of sharing information among team members. Some teams use a communication log; others use short team meetings. Whatever communication mode your program uses, it will be effective only if everyone uses it as intended.

- **Assume others have good intentions.** When communicating about a problem or concern, start with the assumption that everyone involved has good intentions—even if errors have occurred. This positive point of view will help you focus on solutions rather than blame.

- **Ask questions and be prepared to listen.** Communicate *with* others, not *at* them. Remember that you can learn as much (maybe more) by listening as you can by talking. Being part of a team means that you need to understand and appreciate others' points of view. You cannot do so unless you are prepared to listen to those viewpoints.

- **Acknowledge your errors and ask for help.** No one is perfect— neither you nor your colleagues. When things go wrong (and they will), be prepared to acknowledge that you have made a mistake. And when you are unsure what to do, ask for help. This practice helps you learn and grow as a professional, and it models an open and positive attitude for your colleagues.

- **Take conflicts away from the children.** You may occasionally have a difference of opinion with a colleague. Such issues are best settled away from the children. Disagreements, although a normal part of working with others, can be unsettling to the children and their families.

- **Remember professionalism, ethics, and rules of confidentiality.** While you can share most things with your colleagues on the same team, you shouldn't share everything. For example, you should share personal information about families only with those who truly need to know for the welfare and safety of the children. Sharing information with teammates who do not need to know is unprofessional.

APPLY YOUR KNOWLEDGE

Meet with your Orientation Mentor to gather information about the way your program facilitates team communication. Answer the following questions and complete the task described:

1. What tools, forms, or formats does your program use for sharing information among team members? Where are these tools or forms located, and how should you use them?

_____

_____

_____

2. How and how often is team information updated? How are updates shared?

_____

_____

_____

3. Is electronic communication used to share team information? If so, how and by whom?

_____

_____

_____

4. Take a tour with your Orientation Mentor of the team communication tools used in your program. Look at bulletin boards, communication logbooks, hand-books, and any other tools used for communication among team members.

   Initials _____

☑ CHECK YOUR LEARNING: CHAPTER 3

Answer the following questions about what you have learned in this chapter. When you have completed these questions, check in with your Orientation Mentor.

1. Where would you locate the program's health and safety policies and procedures for future reference?

    _____

    _____

    _____

    _____

2. Describe two best practices for use during arrival time.

    _____

    _____

3. Describe two best practices for bottle-feeding infants.

    _____

    _____

4. Describe three best practices for toddler or preschool meals or snacks.

_____

_____

_____

_____

_____

5. Describe a safe and hygienic diaper-changing procedure.

_____

_____

_____

_____

_____

6. Describe three best practices to support toilet learning.

    _____

    _____

    _____

    _____

    _____

7. Describe three best practices associated with outdoor play.

    _____

    _____

    _____

8. How many minutes before outdoor play should you apply sunscreen?

_____

_____

_____

9. In what position must you lay all infants for sleep?

_____

_____

_____

_____

10. List two things you can do to create an environment that helps calm children and supports safe sleep.

_____

_____

11. Describe three best practices for carrying out developmentally appropriate large- or small-group activities.

_____

_____

_____

CHAPTER 4

Being a Professional

So far, your orientation has focused on the knowledge and skills you will need to be successful in working with children, families, and teammates. In this final chapter, the focus is on your most important teaching tool: you. Teachers rely on their minds and bodies to develop and carry out the strategies that support children's development. Like any professional, you must maintain your tools to be effective in your work. Keeping your mind and body in shape is as important to your teaching as maintaining woodworking tools is to a carpenter's craft.

Professionalism

Working with children is an important, although sometimes undervalued, profession. People who do not understand your work may think it is easy. It is actually complex, mentally challenging, and physically demanding work that requires you to be in top-notch shape to be effective. Professionals in early childhood programs take their work seriously, and therefore they take time to ensure that they are physically and mentally prepared for its rigors.

Personal Appearance

You may have heard the saying "Don't judge a book by its cover." Despite this well-known advice, publishers spend a great deal of time and money designing book covers because they know that people do make judgments based on appearances. Such judgments apply not only to books but also to teachers. Children, their families, and your colleagues will form impressions of you as a professional based on your appearance. So, what image do you want to project?

Most early childhood professionals hope to project an image of confidence, professionalism, and trustworthiness. Teachers also want to convey that they are fun-loving and ready to interact actively with children in playful games, messy artwork, and the other pursuits of daily learning. The following guidelines can help you make good decisions about your appearance on the job:

- **Follow the dress code or personal appearance rules for your program.** Most programs have some kind of dress code describing the types of clothes, jewelry, and other appearance items that are permitted and prohibited. Following the dress code shows that you are a professional and a team player.

- **Put yourself in the families' shoes.** Families trust you with their most valued treasures, their children. Sometimes family members know little about you besides how you look when they first hand over their children. Make it easy for families to trust in your good judgment and commitment to the children by dressing neatly, modestly, and appropriately for the day's activities.

- **Remember that you are a role model.** The children in your care look up to you and see you as a role model. Your appearance should reinforce the idea that you take your job seriously.

- **Consider the weather.** Your work is both indoors and outdoors. You will need to dress for the weather and for a wide range of activities. In cold weather you will need a hat, boots, a warm coat, and gloves for outdoor play. In summer you will need sunscreen, lightweight but modest clothing, and a sun hat and sunglasses.

- **Prepare for action.** Your job is an active one. You must dress to run, jump, and climb as well as sit on the floor and hold children in your lap. Short skirts or short shorts, high heels, flip-flops, and similar clothing are not conducive to active teaching.

- **Eliminate heavy scents.** Excessive perfumes or the smell of cigarette smoke can be distasteful and even dangerous for young children. Most programs prohibit smoking on the premises, but smoke from home or the car can linger on your clothes, hair, and body. Do not let your personal habits hinder your appearance or put children's health at risk.

Professional Behavior

Appearances are important, but it is not enough to simply look professional. Your behavior must also show that you are a prepared and trustworthy professional. Professionals share a set of behaviors that set them apart from others who are simply doing a job. To be a true professional, you must demonstrate the following behaviors:

- **Be on time.** Your presence in the classroom is critical. The children and your colleagues are counting on you, so it is essential that you arrive on time and prepared to work at the beginning of your scheduled shift. If an emergency occurs that will cause you to be absent or late, notify your program as soon as possible using the established procedure.

- **Plan ahead.** There may be times when you know you must miss a day of work. Be courteous and notify the program as early as possible using the established procedure for requesting time off.

- **Bring a positive attitude to work.** All teachers have days when they feel down or out of sorts. Professionals put these feelings aside and focus on the needs of the children and the program. You may find that when you decide to act happy and positive, you actually start feeling happier and more positive.

- **Follow procedures for resolving differences or voicing concerns.** Occasionally you may not understand or may disagree with a procedure, a policy, or a practice of the program. You should voice your concerns professionally, using the program's established procedure. If a written procedure does not exist, it is generally safe to assume that you should bring your concerns directly to your supervisor, not to your colleagues or to the children's families.

- **Avoid participating in gossip.** Professionals do not engage in inappropriate communication, such as spreading rumors, gossiping, or sharing confidential information. Remember your ethical commitment and your image as a positive, trustworthy professional. Rumormongering and gossiping are not consistent with either of these goals.

Taking Care of You

Working with young children is a rigorous and demanding job. You will be standing for long periods of time, lifting, running, climbing, bending, and stretching. Maintaining this level of physical activity for many hours each day and many days each week requires that you take care of your body. Professionals prepare physically for the rigors of work by following these guidelines:

- **Eat healthy foods.** Your body needs high-quality fuel to work well. Eating a healthy diet is the best way to ensure that your body is well fueled for the work of the day. A full course on nutrition is beyond the scope of this orientation, but generally a healthy diet includes more fruits and vegetables and fewer fats, sugars, and processed foods.

- **Get enough sleep.** Your body (and mind) must be well rested to do the physical and emotional work of this profession. Make a full night of sleep (seven to eight hours) a priority. When you do not get enough sleep, you are more likely to be irritable, short-tempered, and prone to illness or injury. When you are rested, you can enjoy the work of the day and see humor in the bumps in the road.

- **Recognize signs of stress.** Everyday life comes with some stresses. Working with children presents some additional unique stresses because children can be unpredictable and demanding. When you feel stress building, use the stress-reducing strategies described in chapter 2.

- **Use your break to recharge.** Most programs provide a break for teachers at some point during the day. This break is designed to give you some time away from the job to refresh and recharge your mind and body. During your break, leave the classroom (provided that children are properly supervised) and consider taking a short walk, getting a drink of water, or relaxing with a good book.

- **Drink water.** Your body and brain need water to function well. Sip water throughout the day. Do not wait until you feel thirsty to take a drink, and do not substitute soda or coffee for water. Caffeinated beverages do not hydrate you. They actually have the opposite effect.

- **Get routine medical care, including immunizations.** Like any tool, your body needs routine maintenance. See your doctor for routine physicals and maintain your immunity with immunizations.

- **Report injuries and illnesses.** If you have been injured on the job or become ill, report this immediately to your supervisor. This allows your supervisor to arrange coverage for your classroom while you seek medical treatment. Even if you do not feel you need immediate medical treatment, notify your supervisor so she can be prepared if your situation worsens.

- **Enjoy your day.** Working with young children is not easy, but it is fun. Take time during the day to notice the children's joy in learning and their many accomplishments. Laugh often with the children and participate in some of the playful activities alongside them.

APPLY YOUR KNOWLEDGE

Meet with your Orientation Mentor to gather information about how your program can support your professionalism. Answer the following questions:

1. What is the dress code or personal appearance code for the program? Where is it located?

   _____

   _____

   _____

   _____

2. What is the procedure for notifying the program if you will be unavoidably late or absent?

   _____

   _____

   _____

   _____

3. What is the procedure for requesting time off? Who approves time off, and how much notice is required?

   _____

   _____

   _____

4. What is the procedure for voicing concerns or disagreements?

   _____

   _____

   _____

5. How does your program handle breaks?

_____

_____

_____

_____

_____

6. If you need an unscheduled break, how does your program handle that need?

_____

_____

_____

_____

_____

7. How should you report injuries that occur during the day?

_____

_____

_____

_____

8. If you become ill during your shift, how should you handle this?

_____

_____

_____

_____

Continuing Your Learning

In addition to preparing physically, emotionally, and mentally for each day's work, professionals plan for their ongoing education. This orientation is just the beginning of your professional learning journey. When this orientation is complete, you will still have many, many things to learn about the care and education of young children.

The regulations governing your early childhood program may require that you have ongoing education or training. These requirements exist because research shows that professionals who participate in ongoing professional development do a better job addressing the needs of young children and supporting their development.

Even if your program doesn't require ongoing professional development or training, you would still benefit from participating. Ongoing professional development is important for the following reasons:

- **Practices in early childhood change over time.** We are constantly learning new things about how best to support children's development. Participation in ongoing professional development helps ensure that you keep up with the latest ideas and research findings in your profession.

- **Professional development helps you be better at your work.** Professional development helps you improve your skills. When you are better at your work, it is easier and more enjoyable.

- **Professional development builds your team.** Many programs use professional development as a way for colleagues to get to know one another outside of the everyday work and to build relationships as teammates. When you are part of a strong, cohesive team, your work is easier and more fun.

Professional development can take many forms. You might have the opportunity to take classes, attend workshops, or participate in other training sessions as part of your ongoing professional development. Your program may provide some of your ongoing professional development in the form of team meetings or other on-site activities. Many early childhood professionals continue to learn and grow professionally by subscribing to and reading journals and books related to child development and child care. The resources section of this book may be a good starting place for your ongoing development. You can also develop informally as a professional by reflecting on and learning from everyday events.

Everyday Reflection and Learning

Every day you work in an early childhood program presents abundant learning opportunities for the children and for you, too. Take advantage of these learning opportunities by reflecting each day on the successes and challenges of your work. Some teachers use a journal to write about each day's learning; others simply spend a few minutes in thought at the end of the day.

Whether you choose to write about your teaching journey or mull it over in your mind, think of this time as a learning experience. What did you learn from the things that went well? What did you learn from the things that did not go well? What might you try in the future based on what you have learned? These questions will help you use reflection to consistently improve your teaching practices.

In some programs, teachers have time together each week or month to discuss reflections on their teaching practices. In these programs, teachers share ideas about successes and challenges. Teachers also share suggestions and plan new ideas to improve their work. Gathering informally with other teachers on a regular basis is a useful strategy to learn from your reflections on your work.

Professional Development Planning

Informal reflection on your work is a wonderful tool for improving your practice. A more formal plan for your ongoing professional development is another important strategy. In your plan you will need to establish goals by deciding what you want to accomplish and identifying activities that will help you do so. For example, you may want to advance to a lead teaching position. To do so, you may need to take several credit-based classes or obtain a credential such as the Child Development Associate (CDA). Or your goals may be more modest. You may want to become certified in first aid and CPR. Taking first aid and CPR classes and passing the certification test would help you meet your goal. Regardless of the breadth or complexity of your professional goals, having a plan will help you ensure that you reach them.

Your program may have a professional development plan for your use. Or you can create a simple plan using a format like the one below. The look of the plan is less important that its contents. An effective plan should describe your goal, the activities you will complete to meet the goal, and the timeline (due dates) for conducting those activities.

Professional Goal	Activities to Achieve Your Goal	Timeline	Accomplished?
1.			
	_____	_____	_____
	_____	_____	_____
2.			
	_____	_____	_____
	_____	_____	_____

APPLY YOUR KNOWLEDGE

Meet with your Orientation Mentor to gather information about the way your program facilitates ongoing professional development. Answer the following questions and complete the task described:

1. What ongoing professional development does your program require?

2. How does your program schedule and carry out team meetings?

3. How does your program handle professional development planning?

4. What professional development resources exist to support ongoing learning and career growth?

5. Review your professional development plan with your Orientation Mentor. Select one goal and several activities for achieving the goal, and start doing these activities.

   Initials _____

✓ CHECK YOUR LEARNING: CHAPTER 4

Answer the following questions about what you have learned in this chapter. When you have completed these questions, check in with your Orientation Mentor.

1. Describe two guidelines for a professional appearance.

_____

_____

2. Describe two guidelines for professional behavior on the job.

_____

_____

3. Describe two ways to keep yourself mentally and physically healthy for your work.

_____

_____

4. Why is ongoing professional development important?

_____

_____

_____

_____

Congratulations! Your initial orientation is complete. You are now ready to work with your Orientation Mentor to identify the next steps on your professional journey. Welcome to the profession.

RESOURCES

To learn more about the topics in this orientation guide, access the following resources:

American Academy of Pediatrics. 2015. "A Child Care Provider's Guide to Safe Sleep." www.healthychildren.org/English/family-life/work-play /Pages/A-Child-Care-Provider's-Guide-to-Safe-Sleep.aspx.

American Academy of Pediatrics, American Public Health Association, and National Resource Center for Health and Safety in Child Care and Early Education. 2011. *Caring for Our Children: National Health and Safety Performance Standards; Guidelines for Early Care and Education Programs, Third Edition.* http://cfoc.nrckids.org/WebFiles/CFOC3_updated_final.pdf.

Bergen, Sharon, and Rachel Robertson. 2013. *Healthy Children, Healthy Lives: The Wellness Guide for Early Childhood Programs.* Saint Paul, MN: Redleaf Press.

California Childcare Health Program. 2006. "Preventing and Managing Illness in ECE Programs." www.ucsfchildcarehealth.org/pdfs/Curricula /CCHA/9_CCHA_IllnessPrev_0506.pdf.

———. 2007. "Health and Safety in the Child Care Setting: Prevention of Injuries. A Curriculum for the Training of Child Care Providers: Module 2, Second Edition." www.ucsfchildcarehealth.org/pdfs/Curricula/Prev _Injuries_052407.pdf.

Center for Inclusive Child Care (CICC). 2015. "Quick Links." www.inclusivechildcare.org.

Centers for Disease Control and Prevention. 2015. "Developmental Milestones." www.cdc.gov/ncbddd/actearly/milestones.

Copple, Carol, and Sue Bredekamp, eds. 2009. *Developmentally Appropriate Practice in Early Childhood Programs.* Washington, DC: NAEYC. The position statement and resources related to this book are available online at www.naeyc.org/DAP.

Epstein, Ann S. 2014. *The Intentional Teacher: Choosing the Best Strategies for Young Children's Learning*, rev. ed. Washington, DC: NAEYC.

Harvard University. Center on the Developing Child. http://developingchild .harvard.edu.

National Association for the Education of Young Children. 2005. "NAEYC Code of Ethical Conduct and Statement of Commitment." www.naeyc .org/files/naeyc/file/positions/PSETH05.pdf. Additional resources supporting the use of the code are available online at www.naeyc.org /ethics.

———. 2009. "Position Statement on Prevention of Child Abuse." www.naeyc.org/positionstatements/prevention.

———. 2015. "NAEYC Early Childhood Program Standards and Accreditation Criteria & Guidance for Assessment." www.naeyc.org/files/academy/file/ AllCriteriaDocument.pdf.

Technical Assistance Center on Social Emotional Intervention for Young Children (TACSEI). 2011. "Challenging Behavior." http://challengingbehavior.fmhi.usf.edu.

University of Minnesota. 2015. Center for Early Education and Development (CEED). "Tip Sheets." www.cehd.umn.edu/CEED/publications/tipsheets /default.html.

US Department of Health and Human Services. 2008. "The Role of Professional Child Care Providers in Preventing and Responding to Child Abuse and Neglect." www.childwelfare.gov/pubPDFs/childcare.pdf.

Washington, Valora, ed. 2013. *Essentials for Working with Young Children*. Washington, DC: Council for Professional Recognition.

REFERENCES

AAP (American Academy of Pediatrics). 2015. "Abusive Head Trauma (Shaken Baby Syndrome)." www.aap.org/en-us/about-the-aap/aap -press-room/aap-press-room-media-center/Pages/Abusive-Head-Trauma -Fact-Sheet.aspx.

AAP, APHA, and NRC (American Academy of Pediatrics, American Public Health Association, and National Resource Center for Health and Safety in Child Care and Early Education). 2011. *Caring for Our Children: National Health and Safety Performance Standards; Guidelines for Early Care and Education Programs, Third Edition.* http://cfoc.nrckids.org /WebFiles/CFOC3_updated_final.pdf.

CDC (Centers for Disease Control and Prevention). 2015. "Sudden Unexpected Infant Death and Sudden Infant Death Syndrome: About SUID and SIDS." www.cdc.gov/sids/aboutsuidandsids.htm.

Copple, Carol, and Sue Bredekamp. 2006. *Basics of Developmentally Appropriate Practice: An Introduction for Teachers of Infants and Toddlers.* Washington, DC: NAEYC.

Epstein, Ann S. 2014. *The Intentional Teacher: Choosing the Best Strategies for Young Children's Learning*, rev. ed. Washington, DC: NAEYC.

Lederer, Richard. 2011. *A Tribute to Teachers: Wit and Wisdom, Information and Inspiration about Those Who Change Our Lives.* Portland, OR: Marion Street Press.

NAEYC (National Association for the Education of Young Children). 2009. "Position Statement: Developmentally Appropriate Practice in Early Childhood Programs Serving Children from Birth through Age 8." www .naeyc.org/files/naeyc/file/positions/PSDAP.pdf.

———. 2011. "Code of Ethical Conduct and Statement of Commitment." www.naeyc.org/files/naeyc/image/public_policy/Ethics%20Position%20Statement2011_09202013update.pdf.

NAEYC and NACCRRA (National Association for the Education of Young Children and National Association of Child Care Resource and Referral Agencies). 2011. "Early Childhood Education Professional Development: Training and Technical Assistance Glossary." NAEYC. www.naeyc.org/GlossaryTraining_TA.pdf.

Robertson, Connie, ed. 1998. *Dictionary of Quotations*, 3rd ed. Ware, UK: Wordsworth Editions.

US Department of Health and Human Services, Administration for Children and Families, Administration on Children, Youth and Families, Children's Bureau. 2010. "The Child Abuse Prevention and Treatment Act." www.acf.hhs.gov/sites/default/files/cb/capta2010.pdf.

———. 2015. "Child Maltreatment 2013." www.acf.hhs.gov/sites/default/files/cb/cm2013.pdf.

Certificate of Achievement

THIS CERTIFICATE IS PRESENTED TO

_____

FOR COMPLETING THE *EARLY CHILDHOOD STAFF ORIENTATION GUIDE.*

_____

SHARON BERGEN

Redleaf Press®